A Vegan Taste of the
Caribbean

Linda Majzlik

JON CARPENTER

Our books may be ordered from bookshops or (post free in the UK) from
Jon Carpenter Publishing, Alder House, Market Street, Charlbury,
England OX7 3PH

Please send for our free catalogue

Credit card orders should be phoned or faxed to 01689 870437
or 01608 811969

First published in 2001 by
Jon Carpenter Publishing
Alder House, Market Street, Charlbury, England OX7 3PH
☎ 01608 811969

ISBN 1 897766 70 X

Printed in England by J. W. Arrowsmith Ltd., Bristol

CONTENTS

CONTENTS

Contents

INTRODUCTION

Stretching from Florida to Venezuela, the West Indian islands are spread across 2000 miles of the Caribbean Sea, separating it from the Atlantic Ocean. The islands enjoy a hot tropical climate well suited to growing exotic fruits and vegetables.

Caribbean cuisine is impossible to define, for the simple reason that it has been influenced by the many rich and varied cultures that have inhabited or claimed ownership of the islands over the years. The first inhabitants of many of the islands were tribes of American Indians, the Arawaks and Caribs. They are believed to have been the first to cultivate hot peppers, sweet potatoes, pumpkin, maize and some tropical fruits and nuts. With the arrival of the Spaniards in the 15th century came the introduction of new foods, most notably citrus fruits, tamarind, coconut, bananas, grapes, sugar cane, ginger, date and figs. Rice and peas, a dish which in various forms is traditional all over the Caribbean, is thought to be an adaptation of a Spanish dish.

Evidence of the British influence on the cuisine shows in popular favourites such as porridge, jams and marmalades, Christmas pudding, tarts, buns and pastries, Irish potatoes, rice pudding and black pudding. Spicy Jamaican patties are thought to be derived from the Cornish pasty. In the 16th century large numbers of African slaves were brought to the islands to work on the sugar plantations. Their influence on the methods of cooking and the ingredients still used today was considerable. The Africans brought with them yam, coco, peanuts, plantains, okra, gungo peas and ackee and they prepared mainly one-pot meals. The tradition of one-pot meals continues, with many main course soups, stews and rice dishes being cooked in a large round-bottomed pot called a duchy or Dutch pot.

After the abolition of slavery in the 19th century Chinese and East Indians were brought to the Caribbean as indentured labourers. The Chinese introduced soy sauce, noodles, spices and Chinese vegetables, which were cooked in a wok. The Indians used a karahi – a concave pot similar to a wok – and brought with them more spices, curries, chutneys, mangoes, wheatflour, rice, aubergines, lettuce, cucumber, green beans and cabbage.

Caribbean cooking today is a fascinating, colourful and vibrant mixture of the many styles which have been introduced over the centuries. Where else in the world could you find macaroni, black pudding, chow mein, stuffed puris, gumbo and jerk sitting happily on the same menu? With the abundant use of fresh fruit and vegetables, grains, nuts and pulses in the Caribbean diet, there's plenty of scope for vegan cooks to sample this culinary adventure.

THE VEGAN CARIBBEAN STORECUPBOARD

In addition to the following storecupboard ingredients, some Caribbean vegetables also have a long shelf life. These include pumpkin, squash, christophene, yam, sweet potato, eddo and coco. If stored in a dark, dry, airy cupboard they will keep for several weeks.

Ackee Introduced from West Africa, the ackee is the fruit of the evergreen blighia sapida tree. The creamy-coloured flesh is the edible portion and it is unlike any other fruit in taste or looks. Ackee combines well with vegetables in savoury dishes and is available tinned in salt water. It needs to be drained and rinsed before use.

Agar agar A vegan gelling compound made from various types of seaweed. Used as an alternative to gelatine when making fruit jellies.

Almonds Toasted flaked almonds make a nutritious and tasty addition to stir-fried vegetables, whilst ground and flaked almonds are an essential in some dessert recipes.

Beans and peas A variety of beans and peas are popular all over the Caribbean and are used in soups, stews, rice dishes and salads. Black-eye beans, black and red kidney beans, chickpeas, pigeon or gunga peas and split peas are available tinned or dried. It is worth cooking beans in bulk as they can be frozen successfully.

Breadcrumbs Used for toppings, stuffings and puddings, breadcrumbs can be stored in the freezer and used from frozen.

Cashew nuts A member of the pulse family, the cashew tree is similar to a large apple tree and it grows in parts of the Caribbean. A good source of protein and minerals, cashews are used in both sweet and savoury dishes.

Cheese Cheese does not feature much in Caribbean cuisine. However, it is an essential ingredient in macaroni cheese-type dishes and it is used to garnish Mediterranean-style rice dishes. Vegan 'cheddar' substitutes are used in the recipes here.

Coconut Not a true nut, but the fruit of the coconut palm which grows all over the Caribbean region. Used in various forms, coconut adds richness and flavour to sweet and savoury dishes.

Creamed This is pure fresh coconut flesh shaped into a vacuum-packed block. Once opened the block needs to be kept in the fridge and used within a couple of weeks.

Desiccated The dried flesh of the coconut is popular in baking, pudding and drinks recipes.

Flaked Flakes of dried coconut flesh can be used to garnish both sweet and savoury dishes. Lightly toasting the flakes enhances the flavour.

Milk A rich thick liquid made from pressed coconut flesh, this is available tinned or in cartons. Coconut milk can also be made by dissolving 4oz/100g grated creamed coconut in 20 fl.oz/600ml hot water, or by blending 6oz/175g desiccated coconut with 20 fl.oz/600ml hot water and straining it through a fine sieve or muslin bag, pressing out as much liquid as possible. Any unused coconut milk can be frozen.

Cornflour A very fine starchy white flour which is milled from corn. It is some-times known as cornstarch and is used for thickening.

Cornmeal Ground yellow maize, also known as polenta or maizemeal. Cornmeal is milled in many grades from fine to coarse and is used in sweet and savoury recipes and for making cornbread and dumplings.

Ginger, root It is widely believed that the best ginger is grown in Jamaica, so it naturally features in lots of Caribbean dishes. Root ginger is used in hot spicy dishes, curries and marinades and in drinks. To store root ginger, cut into portions, wrap individually in foil and freeze.

Ginger, stem Stem ginger preserved in sugar syrup is available in jars. This sweetened version is used in desserts and in baking, especially the famous Jamaican ginger cake. The ginger syrup can be added to fruit salads or spooned over ice cream or pancakes.

Golden syrup Sweet and delicate in taste, this thick syrup is made from molasses residue that has been clarified. Useful for baking and dessert recipes where the taste of molasses is not required.

Herbs With the exception of thyme not many herbs are used in Caribbean cookery. The herbs that are used only fresh can be grown in pots on the kitchen windowsill and a few leaves cut off as required.

Bay leaves These dark green, aromatic leaves from an evergreen tree are best used dried to impart their distinct, strong and slightly bitter flavour. They are used in soups and stews.

Chives Fresh chives are often used as a garnish for salads.

Coriander Fresh coriander leaves are used for garnishing.

Mixed herbs A mixture of several sweet herbs and an essential flavouring for split pea pudding.

Parsley This universally popular herb is used in various savoury dishes and it combines well with other herbs. Fresh parsley is also used for garnishing.

Thyme Numerous varieties of thyme are grown around the world, but the type favoured in the Caribbean has a large thick leaf. It is without doubt the most popular herb in the region, but unfortunately it is rarely available outside the Caribbean so the small-leaved thymes have to be used as a substitute.

Hot pepper sauce A mixture of Scotch bonnet and habanero peppers, this sauce gives an authentic taste to Caribbean dishes but it needs to be used sparingly.

Lentils Red lentils are used in many soup and stew recipes and they do not need soaking before cooking. They combine well with other ingredients and are sometimes cooked with rice.

Macaroni Macaroni cheese-type dishes are a favourite in many parts of the Caribbean. Small macaroni shapes can also be added to cook-up soups.

Molasses A very dark, richly flavoured, treacly syrup which is a by-product of the sugar-making process. It is a rich source of iron, vitamins and minerals and is an essential ingredient in rich fruit cakes.

Noodles Introduced from the Far East, noodles are added to soups and used in the ever-popular chow mein dishes. Some noodles contain eggs so be sure to read the label before buying.

Peanuts A good source of protein, vitamins and minerals, roasted peanuts are used ground as an ingredient or chopped or whole as a garnish.

Peanut butter Smooth and crunchy versions are used in dishes with an African influence.

Rice Since being cultivated by the East Indian immigrants, rice has become a staple food in the Caribbean. Long grain white rice is the most popular type and is served either plain or flavoured with herbs, spices, beans and vegetables. Basmati is more expensive, but it gives an authentic flavour to East Indian-influenced dishes.

Rum Jamaican rum is widely regarded as being the best rum in the world and it forms the basis of countless cocktails and punches. It is also used to flavour rich fruit cakes and ice creams. Dark, white or golden varieties are available.

Scotch bonnet pepper The Scotch bonnet pepper is the hottest variety known and should be used very sparingly. So called because of their resemblance to little bonnets, these fiery peppers vary in colour from pale yellow to bright green and red. They are available fresh or bottled. Fresh peppers can be stored in the fridge for several days.

Soy sauce Introduced by the Chinese, soy sauce finds its way into numerous savoury dishes, salad dressings and marinades. Look for naturally fermented varieties rather than those that contain flavourings and colourings.

Spices A whole host of spices are grown in the Caribbean region and naturally enough these are put to good use to impart their unique flavours to sweet and savoury dishes.

Allspice Tasting of a mixture of cinnamon, cloves and nutmeg, allspice is the dried berry of an evergreen tree grown in the Caribbean region and Central America. Allspice is also known as pimento, Jamaica pepper or Jamaica pimento. It is used extensively in sweet and savoury dishes and is available whole or ground.

Black pepper An essential seasoning in all savoury dishes. Coarsely ground black peppercorns are preferred to ready-ground pepper.

Cayenne pepper The dried fruit of a pepper plant which is native to the Caribbean, cayenne is deep red in colour and has a pungent, very hot flavour.

Chilli Dried chilly powder is very hot and should be used sparingly. Dried whole chilli pods are often added to soups and stews and removed before serving.

Cinnamon The dried inner bark of a tree in the laurel family. The highly pungent yet comforting, mild sweet flavour makes it a popular spice to add to sweet and savoury dishes. Cinnamon is available in sticks or ground.

Cloves The name cloves comes from the French word 'clou', meaning nail, which is exactly what a whole clove looks like. Ground cloves are used for flavouring rich fruit cakes and other sweet dishes.

Coriander The dried seed of a plant which belongs to the parsley family. Coriander is a popular Indian spice and is an ingredient in curry powders and garam masala. Used in savoury and sweet dishes, coriander has a mild sweet orangey flavour.

Cumin Sometimes called jeera in the Caribbean, cumin is available as whole seeds or ground. It has a strong earthy flavour and is one of the spices in curry powder.

Curry powder/paste A blend of several different spices, usually cumin, coriander, chilli, ginger, cardamom, turmeric and cinnamon. Caribbean curried dishes tend to be less hot than the East Indian varieties, so choose mild curry powder mixes and pastes.

Five-spice powder A mixture of cinnamon, cloves, fennel, pepper and star anise with a very strong, piquant flavour, which is used sparingly in Chinese-style dishes.

Ginger The dried root is light beige in colour with a strong, spicy sweet flavour, ideally suited to sweet dishes. It is also an ingredient in some curry powder mixes.

Mace The hard, lacy outer covering of the nutmeg kernel, mace and nutmeg are the only two spices to come from the same tree. Mace has a similar but milder flavour to nutmeg and can be used as a substitute for it.

Nutmeg The sweet and spicy seed of an evergreen tree grown in the Caribbean. Nutmeg is available as whole seeds for grating or ready ground. It is used sparingly to flavour puddings and cakes and occasionally savoury dishes.

Paprika The dried pod of a sweet red pepper which is native to Central America. Mild and slightly sweet in flavour, paprika is added to soups and stews and other savoury dishes.

Saffron The most expensive of all the spices available, saffron is made from the dried stigmas of a variety of crocus. Bright yellowy/orange in colour, saffron is used sparingly to impart its colour and pungent, slightly bitter, yet aromatic taste, especially in rice dishes.

Turmeric This tropical plant belongs to the ginger family and is Asian in origin. The bright yellow spice is the powdered rhizome of the plant and is used for colouring and flavouring, in particular rice dishes.

Tamarind The fruit of a large tropical tree, tamarind is used to add sourness to savoury dishes and drinks. It is usually sold in a sticky block consisting of crushed pods, which needs to be soaked in hot water to produce a purée. Jars of ready-made purée are also available.

Tomato purée Used to strengthen the flavour of and add colour to tomato-based dishes. Tomato purée should be used sparingly – too much can give a slightly acidic taste.

Vegetable oils Groundnut, corn and sunflower are favoured cooking oils, while olive oil is more often used for making dressings.

Vegetable stock There is nothing quite like stock made from fresh vegetables and as it is used in so many recipes it's worth making in bulk and freezing in measured quantities until required. The following recipe makes about 3 pints/1.8 litres: 2 onions, peeled and chopped; 2 sticks of celery, trimmed and sliced; 4 garlic cloves, chopped; 2 carrots, scraped and chopped; 1 red pepper, chopped; 1 sweet potato, peeled and chopped; 1 bay leaf; 1 cinnamon stick; black pepper to season; sprig of fresh thyme; 2 tablespoons chopped fresh parsley; 3½ pints/2.1 litres water. Put all the ingredients into a saucepan and bring to the boil. Cover and simmer for 30 minutes, then strain.

Vinegar Light malt and white wine vinegars are preferred for chutneys and salad dressings.

Yeast Easy-blend dried yeast is used in the recipes requiring yeast. It is simple to use as it does not need to be reconstituted in liquid.

APPETISERS

As well as starters for main course meals, these little appetisers also make useful buffet foods or snacks. Dips are easy to make and popular and are often served with plantain chips. For a light and refreshing starter, serve slices of melon or paw paw garnished with a little French dressing.

Spiced chickpea and peanut dip *(serves 4/6)*

12oz/350g cooked chickpeas

1 onion, peeled and grated

2 garlic cloves, crushed

2 rounded tablespoons peanut butter

1 tablespoon vegetable oil

4 tablespoons water

1 dessertspoon hot pepper sauce

2 teaspoons ground cumin

1 teaspoon ground coriander

½ teaspoon paprika

black pepper

Heat the oil in a saucepan and gently fry the onion and garlic until soft. Add the cumin, coriander and paprika and stir around for a few seconds. Remove from the heat and add the chickpeas. Mash with a potato masher until smooth, add the remaining ingredients and mix thoroughly. Transfer to a serving dish, cover and chill before serving.

Avocado and lime dip *(serves 4/6)*

2 large ripe avocados
juice of 1 lime
hot pepper sauce to taste
black pepper
finely grated lime peel

Cut the avocados in half and remove the stones, then scoop out the flesh and mash it with the lime juice until smooth. Season with black pepper and add hot pepper sauce to taste. Mix well and put in a serving bowl. Garnish with a little grated lime peel.

Plantain chips *(serves 6)*

2 green plantains
vegetable oil
salt (optional)

Peel and thinly slice the plantains. Fry the slices in hot vegetable oil until golden and crisp. Drain on kitchen paper and sprinkle with salt if required. Serve with a savoury dip.

Corn fritters *(serves 4/6)*

8oz/225g sweetcorn kernels

4oz/100g cornmeal

4oz/100g self raising flour

1 onion, peeled and finely chopped

8 fl.oz/225ml water

1 teaspoon thyme

1 dessertspoon soy sauce

black pepper

vegetable oil

Put the sweetcorn, onion, water, thyme and soy sauce in a pan and season with black pepper, bring to the boil, cover and simmer for 5 minutes. Allow to cool slightly, then blend until smooth. Pour into a large bowl and add the cornmeal and flour, mixing thoroughly. Shallow fry rounded dessertspoonfuls of the mixture in hot oil until golden. Drain on kitchen paper and serve with a salad garnish.

Paw paw and citrus cup *(serves 4)*

1 ripe paw paw

1 pink-fleshed grapefuit

1 orange

demerara sugar (optional)

2 tablespoons sherry

finely grated orange peel

Peel the grapefruit and orange and remove all the pith, membranes and pips. Chop the segments and put them in a bowl. Peel the paw paw and remove the seeds, dice the flesh and add to the bowl. Sweeten with a little sugar if necessary, add the sherry and mix carefully. Divide the fruit between 4 sundae glasses. Garnish with a little grated orange peel and chill before serving.

Black pudding *(serves 6)*

8oz/225g cooked black or black-eye beans, mashed

3oz/75g mushrooms, wiped and finely chopped

2oz/50g porridge oats

1oz/25g natural minced textured vegetable protein

1 red onion, peeled and finely chopped

2 garlic cloves, crushed

4 fl.oz/125ml vegetable stock

1 dessertspoon vegetable oil

1 dessertspoon tamarind purée

1 dessertspoon soy sauce

1 teaspoon parsley

½ teaspoon thyme

black pepper

vegan margarine

Add the vegetable protein to the stock, cover and leave for 1 hour.

Heat the oil and gently fry the onion and garlic until softened. Add the mushrooms and fry until the juices begin to run, then remove from the heat. Put the soaked vegetable protein in a sieve and press out any excess liquid, then add it to the pan together with the remaining ingredients apart from the margarine, and mix thoroughly.

Spoon the mixture into a lined and greased 7 inch/18cm square baking tin. Press down firmly and evenly, cover and chill for 2 hours. Spread a little vegan margarine all over the top, then bake in a preheated oven at 200°C/400°F/Gas mark 6 for 35-40 minutes until browned. Carefully turn out of the tin and cut into 6 equal portions. Serve with a salad garnish.

Sautéed peppers with ackee *(serves 4)*

4oz/100g red pepper, sliced

4oz/100g green pepper, sliced

4oz/100g yellow pepper, sliced

4oz/100g orange pepper, sliced

a few slices of Scotch bonnet pepper

4oz/100g ackees, chopped

2 celery sticks, trimmed and finely sliced

1 onion, peeled and sliced

2 garlic cloves, crushed

2 tablespoons vegetable oil

1 rounded teaspoon tamarind purée

1 teaspoon soy sauce

black pepper

shredded crisp lettuce

chopped fresh parsley

Gently fry the red, green, yellow, orange and Scotch bonnet peppers, celery, onion and garlic in the oil for about 15 minutes until soft, stirring frequently to prevent sticking. Remove from the heat and stir in the tamarind purée and soy sauce, season with black pepper and put in the fridge until cold. Add the chopped ackees to the pepper mixture and mix well. Arrange some shredded lettuce on 4 serving dishes, pile the salad mixture on top and garnish with chopped fresh parsley.

Peanut- and bean-stuffed tomatoes *(serves 4)*

4 tomatoes

shredded lettuce

chopped fresh parsley

filling

4oz/100g cooked black-eye beans, mashed

2oz/50g peanuts, ground

2oz/50g mushrooms, wiped and finely chopped

4 spring onions, trimmed and finely chopped

2 garlic cloves, crushed

1 dessertspoon vegetable oil

1 teaspoon parsley

½ teaspoon paprika

black pepper

Cut the tomatoes in half. Remove the insides, strain off the juice and chop the flesh. Pat the 8 tomato shells dry with kitchen paper.

Heat the oil in a pan and fry the mushrooms, spring onions and garlic until softened. Add the chopped tomato flesh and cook until pulpy. Remove from the heat, add the remaining filling ingredients and mix very well. Spoon the filling into the tomato halves, cover and keep in the fridge until cold. Put some shredded lettuce on each of 4 plates together with 2 tomato halves garnished with chopped fresh parsley.

Spicy aubergine and bean puris *(serves 8)*

8oz/225g self raising flour

2 tablespoons vegetable oil

¼ teaspoon salt

approx. 4 fl.oz/125ml cold water

extra vegetable oil

filling

10oz/300g aubergine, finely chopped

4oz/100g cooked red kidney beans

1 onion, peeled and finely chopped

2 garlic cloves, crushed

2 tablespoons vegetable oil

4 fl.oz/125ml vegetable stock

1 teaspoon ground cumin

1 teaspoon ground coriander

¼ teaspoon ground allspice

dash of hot pepper sauce

black pepper

Combine the flour, salt and 2 tablespoonfuls of vegetable oil, then gradually add the water until a soft dough forms. Knead well and chill for 30 minutes.

Heat the oil for the filling in a saucepan and gently fry the aubergine, onion and garlic for 15 minutes, stirring frequently to prevent sticking. Add the remaining ingredients and mix well. Bring to the boil, then lower the heat and cook for 5 minutes whilst stirring. Remove from the heat and leave to cool.

Divide the dough into 8 equal portions. Flatten each one into a round and put a rounded tablespoonful of filling in the centre. Pull the pastry edges towards the middle to enclose the filling, then lightly roll each puri into a circle. Deep fry in hot oil until golden. Drain on kitchen paper before serving with a salad garnish.

Black-eye bean and cashew cakes *(serves 4)*

8oz/225g cooked black-eye beans, mashed

4oz/100g cashew nuts, ground

1oz/25g plain flour

1 onion, peeled and grated

2 garlic cloves, crushed

1 dessertspoon vegetable oil

1 dessertspoon soy sauce

¼ teaspoon cayenne pepper

black pepper

extra vegetable oil

Heat the dessertspoonful of vegetable oil in a large pan and fry the onion and garlic until soft. Remove from the heat and add the mashed beans, ground cashews, flour, soy sauce and cayenne pepper. Season with black pepper and stir thoroughly until everything binds together. Take rounded dessertspoon-fuls of the mixture and roll into balls in the palm of the hand. Slightly flatten these balls and brush them all over with vegetable oil. Put them on an oiled baking tray and bake in a preheated oven at 180°C/350°F/Gas mark 4 for 10 minutes. Carefully turn the cakes over and bake them for 10 minutes more. Serve with a salad garnish and salsa.

SOUPS AND STEWS

Soups and stews form an integral part of the Caribbean diet. Made from tropical vegetables and fruits, lentils and beans, and characteristically flavoured with Caribbean seasonings, soups are served either as starters or as light meals. Richly flavoured stews, brimming with vegetables, are more filling and are usually served with dumplings or floats and with mounds of rice. Cornbread is a traditional accompaniment for both soups and stews.

Pumpkin and orange soup *(serves 4)*

1¼lb/550g pumpkin flesh, chopped
1 onion, peeled and finely chopped
12 fl.oz/350ml fresh orange juice
8 fl.oz/225ml soya milk
1 dessertspoon sunflower oil
½ teaspoon paprika
½ teaspoon ground coriander
¼ teaspoon ground mace
black pepper
finely grated orange peel

Heat the oil in a large pan and gently fry the onion until softened. Add the remaining ingredients apart from the soya milk and grated orange peel, and stir well. Bring to the boil, cover and simmer for about 15 minutes until the pumpkin is soft. Allow to cool slightly, then liquidise until smooth. Return to the rinsed-out pan, add the soya milk and reheat whilst stirring. Garnish each bowl of soup with grated orange peel.

Spicy lentil soup *(serves 4)*

8oz/225g red lentils

1 onion, peeled and chopped

2 garlic cloves, crushed

40 fl.oz/1200ml vegetable stock

½oz/15g creamed coconut

1 tablespoon vegetable oil

1 dessertspoon hot pepper sauce

1 teaspoon curry powder

black pepper

Heat the oil in a large pan and soften the onion and garlic. Add the curry powder and stir around for 1 minute. Now add the lentils, stock, coconut and pepper sauce, season with black pepper and stir well. Bring to the boil, cover and simmer gently for about 20 minutes until the lentils are tender. Allow to cool slightly, then liquidise until smooth. Pour back into the cleaned pan and reheat whilst stirring.

Nutty eddo soup *(serves 4)*

1lb/450g eddo, peeled and diced

2oz/50g cashew nuts, chopped

1 onion, peeled and chopped

1 dessertspoon vegetable oil

1 teaspoon soy sauce

½ teaspoon ground cumin

¼ teaspoon grated nutmeg

black pepper

30 fl.oz/900ml vegetable stock

chopped toasted cashew nuts

Heat the oil in a large pan and gently cook the onion until soft. Stir in the eddo and ground cumin and fry for 1 minute. Add the remaining ingredients apart from the cashews and stir. Bring to the boil, cover and simmer gently until the eddo is tender, about 15 minutes. Leave to cool, then liquidise. Rinse out the pan and reheat the soup whilst stirring. Garnish each bowl of soup with chopped toasted cashew nuts.

Tomato and black-eye bean soup *(serves 4)*

2lb/900g ripe tomatoes, skinned and chopped

8oz/225g cooked black-eye beans

20 fl.oz/600ml vegetable stock

1 onion, peeled and finely chopped

4 garlic cloves, crushed

1 tablespoon vegetable oil

1 dessertspoon tomato purée

1 dessertspoon demerara sugar

1 dessertspoon hot pepper sauce

2 bay leaves

1 teaspoon thyme

black pepper

chopped fresh parsley

Gently fry the onion and garlic in the oil in a large pan. Add the tomatoes and cook until pulpy. Now add the remaining ingredients except the parsley and stir well. Bring to the boil, cover and simmer for 20-25 minutes, stirring occasionally, until the soup thickens. Garnish each bowl of soup with chopped fresh parsley.

Sweet potato and lentil soup *(serves 4)*

12oz/350g sweet potato, peeled and grated

2oz/50g red lentils

1 onion, peeled and finely chopped

1 dessertspoon vegetable oil

1 dessertspoon soy sauce

1 teaspoon ground coriander

½ teaspoon paprika

¼ teaspoon cayenne pepper

¼ teaspoon ground mace

black pepper

30 fl.oz/900ml vegetable stock

chopped fresh coriander leaves

Heat the oil in a large pan and fry the onion until softened. Add the coriander, paprika, cayenne pepper and mace and stir around for 1 minute. Wash the lentils and add together with the sweet potato, soy sauce and vegetable stock. Season with black pepper and stir well. Bring to the boil, cover and simmer for about 25 minutes until the lentils are soft. Allow to cool slightly then blend half of the soup until smooth. Pour back into the rest of the soup and stir well. Reheat whilst stirring and serve in bowls, garnished with chopped fresh coriander leaves.

Ackee soup *(serves 4)*

1lb 4oz/540g tin of ackees, drained and rinsed

8oz/225g coco or potato, peeled and diced

4oz/100g ripe tomatoes, skinned and chopped

22 fl.oz/650ml vegetable stock

1 onion, peeled and chopped

1 garlic clove, crushed

1 dessertspoon vegetable oil

1 teaspoon hot pepper sauce

½ teaspoon paprika

black pepper

Heat the oil in a large pan and gently fry the onion and garlic. Add the tomatoes and cook until pulpy, then add the coco or potato, stock, pepper sauce, paprika and half of the ackees. Season with black pepper and stir well. Bring to the boil, cover and simmer for approximately 15 minutes until the coco is soft. Allow to cool slightly and liquidise until smooth. Return to the cleaned pan and add the remaining ackees. Gently reheat while stirring.

Coconut and ginger soup *(serves 4)*

4oz/100g creamed coconut, grated

1 large onion, peeled and chopped

2 large garlic cloves, crushed

1 inch/2.5cm piece of root ginger, peeled and finely chopped

40 fl.oz/1200ml vegetable stock

1 tablespoon vegetable oil

¼ teaspoon ground allspice

dash of soy sauce

dash of hot pepper sauce

black pepper

finely sliced spring onions

Gently fry the onion, garlic and ginger in the oil in a large pan until soft. Add the remaining ingredients apart from the spring onions and stir well. Bring to the boil, cover and simmer for 15 minutes, stirring occasionally. Leave to cool slightly, then liquidise until smooth. Rinse the pan and reheat the soup whilst stirring. Garnish each bowl with finely sliced spring onions.

Callaloo soup *(serves 4/6)*

This rich traditional Trinidadian soup serves 6 as a starter or 4 as a main course. To use as a main course serve with floats (see page 42), a savoury rice dish and salad.

> 1lb/450g callaloo or fresh spinach leaves, trimmed and roughly chopped
>
> 1lb/450g coco or potato, peeled and diced
>
> 8oz/225g green banana, peeled and sliced
>
> 8oz/225g okra, topped, tailed and sliced
>
> 1 onion, peeled and chopped
>
> 4 garlic cloves, crushed
>
> 1oz/25g vegan margarine
>
> 30 fl.oz/900ml vegetable stock
>
> 10 fl.oz/300ml coconut milk
>
> 2 teaspoons parsley
>
> 1 teaspoon thyme
>
> 1 dessertspoon hot pepper sauce
>
> black pepper

Heat the margarine in a large pan and gently fry the callaloo or spinach, onion and garlic for 5 minutes. Add the remaining ingredients, except the coconut milk, and stir well. Bring to the boil, cover and simmer for about 20 minutes until the vegetables are tender. Allow to cool slightly, then liquidise very briefly. Return to the rinsed-out pan and stir in the coconut milk. Bring back to the boil and simmer for a few minutes until heated through.

Cook-up soup *(serves 4)*

Versions of this popular soup are made all over the Caribbean and it is served as a main course rather than a starter. There's no need to be too rigid about the ingredients as it is intended to be the type of dish that uses up whatever is to hand.

    1lb/450g eddo, peeled and diced
    1lb/450g tomatoes, skinned and chopped
    8oz/225g carrot, scraped and thinly sliced
    8oz/225g cooked red kidney beans
    4oz/100g red lentils
    4oz/100g mushrooms, wiped and chopped
    2oz/50g okra, topped, tailed and sliced
    2oz/50g creamed coconut, grated
    1 christophene, peeled and diced
    1 red onion, peeled and finely chopped
    2 garlic cloves, crushed
    2 tablespoons vegetable oil
    48 fl.oz/1425ml vegetable stock
    1 tablespoon hot pepper sauce
    1 teaspoon thyme
    black pepper

Fry the onion and garlic in the oil in a large pan until soft. Add the eddo, carrot, lentils, stock, pepper sauce and thyme and season with black pepper. Stir well, bring to the boil, cover and simmer for 10 minutes. Add the remaining ingredients and again stir well. Cover and simmer for about 25 minutes, until the vegetables are cooked. Serve as a main course with cornmeal dumplings (see page 42), plain boiled rice and salad.

Mixed bean and pepper stew *(serves 4)*

1lb/450g cooked mixed beans (e.g. black-eye, red kidney, gungo, butter)

12oz/350g mixed red, green and yellow peppers, chopped

8oz/225g tomatoes, skinned and chopped

4oz/100g mushrooms, wiped and sliced

1 red onion, peeled and finely chopped

2 garlic cloves, crushed

1 tablespoon vegetable oil

1 rounded dessertspoon tomato purée

1 dessertspoon soy sauce

1 dried red chilli, crumbled

1 teaspoon paprika

1 teaspoon thyme

2 bay leaves

black pepper

24 fl.oz/725ml vegetable stock

finely sliced spring onions

Heat the oil in a large pan and gently fry the onion and garlic until softened. Add the tomatoes, tomato purée and soy sauce and cook until pulpy. Add all remaining ingredients apart from the spring onions and stir well. Bring to the boil, cover and simmer for 30 minutes, stirring occasionally. Garnish with sliced spring onions and serve as a main course with saffron and sweetcorn rice (page 60) and cornbread (page 43).

Groundnut and yam stew *(serves 4)*

1½lb/675g yam, peeled and diced

1lb/450g ripe tomatoes, skinned and finely chopped

8oz/225g carrot, scraped and diced

6oz/175g fine green beans, topped, tailed and cut into 1 inch/2.5cm lengths

3oz/75g natural textured vegetable protein chunks

1 onion, peeled and sliced

1 green chilli, deseeded and finely chopped

1 tablespoon groundnut or sunflower oil

3 rounded tablespoons peanut butter

28 fl.oz/825ml vegetable stock

1 teaspoon turmeric

2 rounded teaspoons ground coriander

2 rounded teaspoons ground cumin

black pepper

roasted peanuts, chopped

Mix the turmeric, coriander and cumin with 20 fl.oz/600ml stock and add the vegetable protein chunks. Stir well, cover and leave for an hour.

Soften the onion and chilli in the oil in a large pan. Cut the soaked vegetable protein chunks in half and add them to the pan together with the remaining soaking stock and the yam, tomatoes and carrot. Stir well and bring to the boil. Cover and simmer gently for 15 minutes, stirring occasionally. Dissolve the peanut butter in the remaining 8 fl.oz/255ml stock and add together with the green beans. Season with black pepper and stir well. Simmer for 15 minutes more until the vegetables are tender, stirring frequently to prevent sticking. Serve as a main course, garnished with chopped roasted peanuts and accompanied by plain boiled rice and fufu (see page 43).

Chickpea gumbo *(serves 4)*

8oz/225g cooked chickpeas

8oz/225g okra, topped, tailed and cut into thick diagonal slices

8oz/225g tomatoes, skinned and chopped

4oz/100g red pepper, sliced

4oz/100g green pepper, sliced

4oz/100g mushrooms, wiped and sliced

1 corn on the cob

2 sticks of celery, trimmed and finely sliced

1 onion, peeled and chopped

4 garlic cloves, crushed

30 fl.oz/900ml vegetable stock

2 tablespoons vegan margarine

2 tablespoons flour

2 tablespoons vegetable oil

1 tablespoon tamarind purée

1 teaspoon thyme

2 teaspoons parsley

2 bay leaves

black pepper

Heat the oil in a large pan and gently fry the onion, celery, garlic and red and green peppers for 10 minutes. Add the tomatoes and cook until pulpy. Cut the corn from the cob and add to the pan together with the okra, stock, tamarind purée, thyme, parsley and bay leaves. Season with black pepper and stir well, then bring to the boil, cover and simmer for 15 minutes.

Melt the margarine in a small saucepan. Add the flour and cook gently for 1 minute. Stir into the gumbo together with the chickpeas and mushrooms and simmer for a further 10 minutes, stirring frequently to prevent sticking. Serve as a main course with coconut rice (see page 61) and salad.

Coconut and veggie one-pot *(serves 4)*

1lb/450 squash, peeled

12oz/350g yam, peeled

12oz/350g sweet potato, peeled

8oz/225g plantain, peeled and sliced

8oz/225g carrot, scraped and sliced

8oz/225g green beans, topped, tailed and cut into 1 inch/2.5cm
   lengths

1 onion, peeled and sliced

20 fl.oz/600ml vegetable stock

4oz/100g creamed coconut, grated

1 dessertspoon vegetable oil

1 dessertspoon hot pepper sauce

¼ teaspoon ground allspice

black pepper

fresh thyme

Cut the squash, yam and sweet potato into even-sized chunks. Heat the oil in a large pan and fry the onion until soft. Add the vegetables and a little vegetable stock, bring to the boil, cover and lower the heat to allow the vegetables to steam for 5 minutes. Combine the coconut, pepper sauce and allspice with the remaining stock, season with black pepper and stir until the coconut dissolves. Mix into the vegetables, bring to the boil, cover and simmer very gently, stirring occasionally, for about 40 minutes until the vegetables are cooked. Garnish with fresh thyme and serve with rice and salad as a main course.

ACCOMPANIMENTS FOR SOUPS, STEWS AND CURRIES

Dumplings are an essential with stews and flour-and-water spinners and cornmeal dumplings are typical of the many varieties made. Both are simmered on top of the stew for about 20 minutes until risen. Alternatively simmer them in vegetable stock for the same amount of time, and then drain and serve separately as a side dish with soups.

Floats are made from a bread-type dough and fried until golden. For the traditional African accompaniment fufu other vegetables such as eddo, sweet potato, yam or plantain can also be used. Warm cornbread is delicious with soup, stews and curries, while roti is generally only served with curries.

Spinners *(serves 4)*

4oz/100g plain flour
pinch of salt
½ teaspoon thyme (optional)
cold water

Mix the flour, salt and thyme and add enough cold water to form a stiff dough. Knead well, then chill for an hour. Roll small pieces of dough into balls about the size of large marbles. Put these on top of the stew and simmer for about 20 minutes.

Cornmeal dumplings *(serves 4)*

4oz/100g self raising flour

2oz/50g fine cornmeal

1oz/25g vegan margarine

½ teaspoon thyme

pinch of salt

soya milk

Put the flour, cornmeal, thyme and salt in a bowl and mix. Rub in the margarine, then add enough soya milk to form a stiff dough. Knead well and chill for 1 hour. Break the dough into small pieces and roll these into balls about the size of large marbles. Place on top of the stew and simmer for about 20 minutes.

Floats *(serves 4)*

8oz/225g plain flour

1 rounded teaspoon easy-blend yeast

pinch of salt

1oz/25g vegan margarine, melted

approx. 4 fl.oz/125ml warm water

vegetable oil

Mix the flour with the yeast and salt and stir in the melted margarine. Gradually add the water until a soft dough forms. Turn out onto a floured board and knead well. Return to the bowl, cover and leave to rise in a warm place for 30 minutes, then knead again. Divide the dough into 16 equal portions and roll each one into a ball. Flatten the balls and again leave in a warm place for 30 minutes. Shallow fry in hot oil for a few minutes each side until golden. Drain on kitchen paper and serve hot.

Fufu *(serves 4)*

1½lb/675g cassava, peeled and diced

Boil the cassava until tender, then drain and mash or pound in a mortar until glutinous. Take rounded dessertspoonfuls and shape into balls, wrap these in foil and put them in a warm oven until heated through.

Cornbread

8oz/225g fine cornmeal

4oz/100g self raising flour

2oz/50g vegan margarine, melted

1oz/25g soya flour

8 fl.oz/225ml soya milk

8 fl.oz/225ml plain soya yoghurt

1 rounded dessertspoon baking powder

1 small red chilli, finely chopped

½ teaspoon salt

Whisk the soya flour with the milk in a large bowl. Add the margarine, yoghurt and chilli and mix well. Gradually add the cornmeal and sifted flour, baking powder and salt. Combine thoroughly, then spoon the mixture into a base-lined and greased 8 inch/20cm loaf tin. Level the top and bake in a preheated oven at 190°C/375°F/Gas mark 5 for about 30 minutes, until the bread is golden and a skewer comes out clean when inserted in the centre. Run a sharp knife around the edges and turn the loaf out onto a wire rack. Cut into slices and serve warm, either plain or spread with vegan margarine.

Roti *(makes 8)*

8oz/225g plain flour
1 rounded teaspoon baking powder
pinch of salt
cold water
melted vegan margarine

Mix the flour, baking powder and salt in a bowl and add enough cold water to form a soft dough. Knead well, then chill for an hour. Divide the dough into 8 equal portions, shape each one into a ball and roll these into 6 inch/15cm diameter circles on a floured board. Heat a heavy-based pan and cook the rotis for a few minutes on each side until brown specks appear. Brush them with a little melted vegan margarine before serving.

MAIN COURSES

This selection of main course dishes illustrates the diverse nature of Caribbean cuisine. The Mediterranean influence is clearly visible in the macaroni bake and stuffed vegetable dishes, but they have been given a unique Caribbean flavour. Jamaican patties, of which there are many variations, are believed to be based on Cornish pasties, while chow mein and Chinese vegetables are very popular. Curried dishes feature too, although the West Indian varieties tend to be milder than their East Indian counterparts, and they are usually served with heaps of rice, roti and salad. The legacy of the African slaves lives on in the jerk method of cooking, jerk being a very hot and spicy marinade.

Jamaican patties *(makes 6)*

pastry

9oz/250g fine wholemeal self raising flour

4oz/100g vegan margarine

½ teaspoon turmeric

water

filling

8oz/225g sweet potato, peeled and finely chopped

4oz/100g tomato, skinned and chopped

2oz/50g minced natural textured vegetable protein

2oz/50g cooked black-eye beans

1 onion, peeled and finely chopped

1 garlic clove, crushed

1 small red chilli, finely chopped

1 tablespoon vegetable oil

1 rounded teaspoon curry powder

black pepper

8 fl.oz/225ml vegetable stock

Mix the turmeric with the flour, rub in the margarine and add enough water to make a firm dough. Cover and refrigerate for 30 minutes.

Heat the oil in a large pan and gently soften the onion, garlic and chilli. Add the tomato and the curry powder and stir around for 1 minute. Stir in the stock, sweet potato and vegetable protein and season with black pepper. Bring to the boil, cover and simmer for about 25 minutes, until the liquid has been absorbed and the potato is tender. Stir frequently to prevent sticking. Remove from the heat and add in the black-eye beans. Allow to cool.

Divide the pastry into 6 equal portions and roll each on out on a floured board into a 6½ inch/16.5cm circle. Divide the filling between the pastry circles, putting it on one side only. Dampen the edges with water, fold the pastry over to enclose the filling and press the edges together. Transfer the patties to a greased baking sheet. Make 3 slits in the top of each one and bake them in a preheated oven at 180°C/350°F/Gas mark 4 for about 30 minutes until golden brown. Serve with vegetables and salad.

Mixed veggie jerk *(serves 4)*

1½ lb/675g prepared mixed vegetables, diced (i.e. sweet potato, yam, peppers, okra, aubergine, courgette)

1lb/450g ripe tomatoes, skinned and chopped

chopped fresh coriander

jerk marinade

1 onion, peeled and finely chopped

4 garlic cloves, crushed

1 green chilli, finely chopped

1 inch/2.5cm piece of root ginger, peeled and finely chopped

2 tablespoons lemon juice

2 tablespoon sunflower oil

1 tablespoon demerara sugar

1 dessertspoon soy sauce

2 teaspoons ground allspice

1 teaspoon ground cinnamon

1 teaspoon thyme

black pepper

Parboil the yam and sweet potato for 10 minutes, drain and put in a large pan with the other diced vegetables. Mix all the marinade ingredients and spoon over the vegetables. Combine well, cover and leave for 2 hours. Then add the tomatoes and bring slowly to the boil whilst stirring. Cover and simmer gently for about 25 minutes until the vegetables are cooked, stirring frequently to prevent sticking. Transfer to a warmed serving dish and garnish with chopped fresh coriander. Serve with a rice dish, salad and cornbread (see page 43).

Chow mein *(serves 4)*

1lb/450g ripe tomatoes, skinned and chopped

8oz/225g jingy or courgette, sliced

8oz/225g green beans, topped, tailed and sliced

4oz/100g red pepper, sliced

4oz/100g thin noodles

4oz/100g mushrooms, wiped and sliced

2oz/50g pak choi, shredded

2oz/50g natural textured vegetable protein chunks

1 onion, peeled and sliced

2 garlic cloves, crushed

1 inch/2.5cm piece of root ginger, peeled and finely chopped

20 fl.oz/600ml vegetable stock

2 tablespoons vegetable oil

1 dessertspoon soy sauce

1 dessertspoon tomato purée

½ teaspoon five spice powder

black pepper

sliced spring onions

Mix the soy sauce and tomato purée with the stock and add the vegetable protein chunks. Stir well, cover and leave for 1 hour.

Gently fry the jingy, red pepper, green beans, mushrooms, pak choi, onion, garlic and ginger for 5 minutes in the oil in a large pan. Cut the soaked vegetable protein chunks in half, add to the pan together with the soaking liquid, tomatoes and five spice powder and season with black pepper, then raise the heat. Cover and simmer for 20 minutes. Add the noodles and stir well, and continue simmering for about 5 minutes until the noodles are done. Garnish with sliced spring onions when serving.

Fruity christophene curry *(serves 4)*

2 christophenes, peeled, stoned and diced

8oz/225g green banana, peeled and chopped

1 medium unripe mango, peeled, stoned and diced

2oz/50g dried dates, chopped

1 inch/2.5cm piece of root ginger, peeled and finely chopped

1 onion, peeled and finely chopped

12 fl.oz/350ml water

4 fl.oz/125ml coconut milk

1 dessertspoon vegetable oil

2 rounded teaspoons mild curry powder

½ teaspoon turmeric

¼ teaspoon ground allspice

1 rounded dessertspoon tamarind purée

1 rounded dessertspoon demerara sugar

black pepper

toasted flaked coconut

Heat the oil in a large pan and fry the onion and ginger until soft. Add the curry powder, turmeric and allspice and stir around for 30 seconds. Dissolve the tamarind purée and sugar in the water and add, together with the christophene. Bring to the boil and simmer gently for about 15 minutes until the christophene is almost tender, then add the green banana, mango, dates and coconut milk and season with black pepper. Stir well and bring back to the boil. Lower the heat and simmer until the fruit is soft and the mixture thickens, stirring frequently. Served in a warmed dish garnished with toasted flaked coconut, with a rice dish, roti (see page 44) and salad.

Stuffed sweet peppers *(serves 4)*

4 sweet peppers

filling

1lb/450g tomatoes, skinned and finely chopped

4oz/100g cooked black-eye beans

4oz/100g sweetcorn kernels

4oz/100g mushrooms, wiped and finely chopped

1oz/25g creamed coconut, grated

1 red onion, peeled and finely chopped

4 garlic cloves, crushed

1 tablespoon vegetable oil

1 teaspoon thyme

1 teaspoon paprika

1 dessertspoon soy sauce

black pepper

topping

½oz/15g breadcrumbs

Cut the peppers in half lengthwise and remove the stalks, membranes and seeds. Put them in a greased shallow casserole dish.

Heat the oil in a large pan and soften the onion and garlic. Add the mushrooms and fry until the juices begin to run, then remove from the heat and add the remaining filling ingredients. Mix thoroughly, fill the pepper halves with this mixture and sprinkle with breadcrumbs. Cover with foil and bake in a preheated oven at 180°C/350°F/Gas mark 4 for 35 minutes. Remove the foil and bake for 5 minutes more until the tops are golden. Serve with rice and salad.

Macaroni bake *(serves 4)*

8oz/225g macaroni

6oz/175g tomatoes, chopped

4oz/100g mushrooms, wiped and chopped

3oz/75g vegan 'cheddar', grated

1 onion, peeled and chopped

18 fl.oz/550ml soya milk

2 dessertspoons cornflour

1 dessertspoon vegetable oil

1 teaspoon thyme

black pepper

2oz/50g breadcrumbs

½ teaspoon ground allspice

Gently fry the onion in the oil in a large pan until softened. Add the mush-rooms and stir around for 30 seconds. Mix the cornflour with the soya milk until smooth, then add together with the 'cheddar' and thyme. Bring to the boil whilst stirring and continue stirring until the sauce thickens. Take off the heat and stir in the tomatoes. Cook the macaroni, drain and add to the sauce. Season with black pepper and mix very well, then spoon into a greased casse-role dish. Mix the ground allspice with the breadcrumbs and sprinkle on top. Cover with foil and bake in a preheated oven at 180°C/350°F/Gas mark 4 for 25 nminutes, then remove the foil and bake for a further 5-10 minutes until browned. Serve with salad.

Baked stuffed cabbage leaves *(serves 4)*

16 large cabbage leaves

8 fl.oz/225ml vegetable stock

filling

8oz/225g carrot, scraped and grated

4oz/100g breadcrumbs

2oz/50g natural minced textured vegetable protein

10 fl.oz/300ml vegetable stock

1 red onion, peeled and finely chopped

2 garlic cloves, crushed

1 tablespoon vegetable oil

1 dessertspoon tomato purée

1 teaspoon mixed herbs

1 teaspoon soy sauce

black pepper

Add the vegetable protein to the 10 fl.oz/300ml stock and leave to stand for 1 hour. Heat the oil and fry the onion, garlic and carrot until soft. Add the soaked vegetable protein and any remaining liquid, together with the tomato purée, mixed herbs and soy sauce. Season with black pepper and stir well. Raise the heat and simmer for 3 minutes. Remove from the heat and add the breadcrumbs, mixing thoroughly.

Trim the hard stems from the cabbage leaves and simmer the leaves for 3 minutes in a large pan of boiling water, then drain them well. Divide the filling equally between the cabbage leaves and roll each leaf up to completely enclose the filling. Put the stuffed leaves in a greased shallow baking dish and pour the 8 fl.oz/225ml of stock over the top. Cover with foil and bake in a preheated oven at 180°C/350°F/Gas mark 4 for 20 minutes. Serve with vegetable accompaniments.

Curried aubergine and potato *(serves 4)*

1lb 2oz/500g aubergine, diced

1lb 2oz/500g potato, peeled and diced

1 onion, peeled and finely chopped

4 garlic cloves, crushed

1 inch/2.5cm piece of root ginger, peeled and finely chopped

8oz/225g tomatoes, skinned and chopped

4 tablespoons sunflower oil

6 fl.oz/175ml vegetable stock

2 rounded teaspoons ground cumin

2 rounded teaspoons ground coriander

½ teaspoon ground allspice

½ teaspoon ground cinnamon

¼ teaspoon cayenne pepper

black pepper

Boil the potatoes for 5 minutes and drain. Heat the oil in a large pan and gently fry the aubergine, onion, garlic and ginger for 15 minutes, stirring frequently to prevent sticking. Add the spices and stir around for another minute, then add the tomatoes and cook until pulpy. Stir in the potatoes and stock and bring to the boil. Cover and simmer for about 15 minutes, until the vegetables are tender and the mixture thickens, adding a little more stock if necessary and stirring frequently. Serve with red rice (see page 61) and salad.

Stuffed baked aubergine *(serves 4)*

2 aubergines, each approx. 12oz/350g

2oz/50g natural minced textured vegetable protein

2oz/50g mushrooms, wiped and chopped

1 red onion, peeled and chopped

2 garlic cloves, crushed

10 fl.oz/300ml vegetable stock

2 tablespoons vegetable oil

1 dessertspoon soy sauce

½ teaspoon ground allspice

black pepper

1oz/25g breadcrumbs

Dissolve the soy sauce and allspice in the stock, add the vegetable protein, cover and leave for 1 hour. Bring a large pan of water to the boil and simmer the aubergines for 5 minutes. Drain and rinse them under cold running water and cut each one in half lengthwise. Scoop out the flesh, leaving shells of about ¼ inch/5mm thick. Put these in an oiled baking dish. Chop the flesh finely and fry it with the onion, garlic and mushrooms in the oil for 10 minutes, stirring frequently. Add the soaked vegetable protein and any remaining liquid and stir well, season with black pepper and bring to the boil. Simmer uncovered for 5 minutes whilst stirring, then spoon the mixture into the aubergine shells and sprinkle the breadcrumbs on top. Cover with foil and bake in a preheated oven at 180°C/350°F/Gas mark 4 for 30 minutes. Remove the foil and return to the oven for about 10 minutes until browned.

Yam and banana korma *(serves 4)*

1½lb/675g yam, peeled and diced

12oz/350g green bananas, peeled and sliced

1 onion, peeled and chopped

1oz/25g creamed coconut, grated

25 fl.oz/750ml hot water

1 tablespoon vegetable oil

2 tablespoons mild curry paste

2 rounded tablespoons natural soya yoghurt

black pepper

garam masala

Dissolve the creamed coconut and curry paste in the hot water. Heat the oil in a large pan and gently fry the onion until softened. Add the curried coconut liquid and the yam to the pan, season with black pepper and bring to the boil. Cover and simmer for 10 minutes, stirring occasionally. Add the banana, stir well and continue cooking until the yam and banana are tender. Take off the heat and stir in the yoghurt, then return to the stove and cook for a couple of minutes whilst stirring. Transfer to a warmed serving dish and garnish with garam masala. Serve with a rice dish and salad.

RICE

Although the African slaves are believed to have been the first to grow rice in the region, it was the East Indian immigrants who began to cultivate it on a large scale. Nowadays, rice is a staple food all over the Caribbean, with great mounds being served with main course dishes and stews. Rice is a relatively cheap food, so it is often used, with the addition of beans and peas, to stretch main course meals. Rice and peas is a good example and so popular is this dish in Jamaica that it is affectionately known as the Jamaican coat of arms. Variations abound and other beans and peas, such as red kidney beans and gungo or pigeon peas, are often used instead of black-eye beans. To produce a fluffier, less sticky end product, most rice benefits from being rinsed in several changes of water, drained and allowed to dry before cooking. Leftover rice dishes can be put in the fridge and served cold as a salad.

Rice and peas *(serves 6)*

1lb/450g long grain rice

12oz/350g cooked black-eye beans

1 green pepper, finely chopped

1 onion, peeled and finely chopped

2 garlic cloves, crushed

2oz/50g creamed coconut, grated

40 fl.oz/1200ml vegetable stock

2 tablespoons sunflower oil

1 teaspoon thyme

black pepper

Heat the oil in a large pan and gently fry the pepper, onion and garlic until softened. Add the rice and stir around for 1 minute. Stir in the remaining ingredients and bring to the boil, then cover and simmer gently for about 15 minutes until the liquid has been absorbed and the rice is cooked. Transfer to a warmed serving dish and fork through before serving.

Sweet pepper and garlic rice *(serves 4)*

8oz/225g long grain rice

6oz/175g red pepper, finely chopped

6oz/175g yellow pepper, finely chopped

4 large garlic cloves, crushed

1 red onion, peeled and finely chopped

20 fl.oz/500ml vegetable stock

1 teaspoon paprika

1 tablespoon finely chopped fresh parsley

2 tablespoons olive oil

black pepper

grated vegan 'cheddar'

4 spring onions, trimmed and finely sliced

Fry the red and yellow peppers, garlic and onion for 10 minutes in the oil in a large pan. Add the rice and paprika and stir around for 1 minute, then the stock and parsley. Season with black pepper, stir well and bring to the boil. Cover and simmer until the liquid has been absorbed and the rice is done. Spoon into a warmed serving dish and garnish with the grated 'cheddar' and spring onions.

Orange, sultana and cashew nut rice *(serves 4)*

8oz/225g basmati rice

2 oranges

2oz/50g sultanas

2oz/50g cashew nuts, toasted

1 onion, peeled and finely chopped

1 tablespoon vegetable oil

½ teaspoon turmeric

black pepper

Cut one of the oranges into slices and keep them for garnish. Squeeze the juice from the other orange, pour it into a measuring jug and make up to 20 fl.oz/600ml with water. Finely grate the peel from the squeezed orange.

Heat the oil in a large pan and fry the onion and grated orange peel until soft. Add the rice and turmeric and stir around for 1 minute. Now add the sultanas and the liquid and season with black pepper. Stir well and bring to the boil, then cover and simmer until the liquid has been absorbed and the rice is cooked. Remove from the heat and stir in the cashew nuts. Transfer to a warmed serving dish and garnish with the orange slices.

Mushroom and chickpea pullau *(serves 6)*

1lb/450g basmati rice

6oz/175g mushrooms, wiped and sliced

6oz/175g cooked chickpeas

1 onion, peeled and finely chopped

2 garlic cloves, crushed

2oz/50g raisins

36 fl.oz/1075ml vegetable stock

1 tablespoon vegetable oil

1 rounded teaspoon ground coriander

½ teaspoon turmeric

2 inch/5cm stick of cinnamon

black pepper

chopped fresh coriander leaves

Gently fry the onion and garlic in the oil until softened. Add the rice, coriander, turmeric and cinnamon and stir around for 1 minute, then add the mushrooms, chickpeas, raisins and stock and season with black pepper. Bring to the boil, cover and simmer gently until the liquid has been absorbed and the rice is tender. Put into a warmed serving dish and garnish with chopped fresh coriander leaves.

Saffron and sweetcorn rice *(serves 4)*

8oz/225g long grain rice

8oz/225g sweetcorn kernels

½oz/15g vegan margarine

1 onion, peeled and finely chopped

1 teaspoon saffron threads

20 fl.oz/600ml vegetable stock

black pepper

Melt the margarine in a large pan and fry the onion with the saffron until soft. Add the rice and stir around for 1 minute. Add the sweetcorn and vegetable stock and season with black pepper, stir well and bring to the boil. Cover and simmer until the liquid has been absorbed and the rice is done.

Red rice *(serves 6)*

1 lb/450g long grain rice

1 red onion, peeled and finely chopped

1 garlic clove, crushed

2 tablespoons vegetable oil

2 rounded tablespoons tomato purée

2 tablespoons water

black pepper

dash of hot pepper sauce

2 tomatoes, sliced

Boil the rice, drain and rinse under cold water. Drain well and put in an oven-proof dish. Dry in a cool oven, stirring frequently to prevent sticking.

Heat the oil in a large pan and gently soften the onion and garlic. Dissolve the tomato purée and pepper sauce in the water and add to the pan together with the rice. Season with black pepper and warm through over a low heat, stirring all the time. Serve in a warmed dish garnished with the tomato slices.

Coconut rice *(serves 4)*

12oz/350g basmati or long grain rice

3oz/75g creamed coconut, grated

30 fl.oz/900ml vegetable stock

black pepper

toasted flaked coconut

Put the rice in a large pan with the creamed coconut and stock. Season with black pepper and bring to the boil. Cover and simmer until the liquid has been absorbed and the rice is done. Put in a warmed serving dish and fork through. Garnish with toasted flaked coconut to serve.

Rice and lentils *(serves 4)*

6oz/175g long grain rice

6oz/175g red lentils

1 onion, peeled and finely chopped

2 garlic cloves, crushed

1 tablespoon vegetable oil

1 rounded dessertspoon tamarind purée

1 dessertspoon parsley

black pepper

28 fl.oz/825ml vegetable stock

4 spring onions, trimmed and finely sliced

Rinse the lentils several times and drain. In a large pan fry the onion and garlic in the oil until softened. Add the rice and lentils and stir around for 1 minute. Dissolve the tamarind purée in the vegetable stock and add to the pan together with the parsley. Season with black pepper, bring to the boil, cover and simmer gently until the liquid has been absorbed and the rice and lentils are cooked. Transfer to a warmed serving dish and garnish with the spring onions.

Cook-up rice *(serves 4)*

Like cook-up soup, this dish is intended to use up whatever vegetables are to hand. Cooked beans or peas are sometimes added and it is served as a main course rather than an accompaniment.

1lb/450g long grain rice

8oz/225g carrot, scraped and finely chopped

6oz/175g fresh spinach, finely chopped

4oz/100g red pepper, finely chopped

1oz/25g mushrooms, wiped and sliced

1oz/25g okra, topped, tailed and sliced

1oz/25g creamed coconut, grated

1 onion, peeled and finely chopped

2 garlic cloves, crushed

1oz/25g vegan margarine

32 fl.oz/950ml vegetable stock

1 dessertspoon hot pepper sauce

1 teaspoon thyme

black pepper

sliced tomatoes to garnish

Fry the carrot, spinach, pepper, mushroom, okra, onion and garlic in the margarine in a large pan for 5 minutes. Add the remaining ingredients apart from the tomatoes and stir well. Bring to the boil, then turn the heat very low, cover and cook for 15-20 minutes until the liquid has been absorbed and the rice and vegetables are tender. Spoon onto warmed plates and garnish with tomato slices. Serve as a main course with salad and chutney or salsa.

VEGETABLE

ACCOMPANIMENTS

*S*hopping for fresh fruit and vegetables from colourful and overladen market stalls is commonplace in most of the Caribbean countries and with such favourable conditions, 'growing your own' is also very popular. Not surprisingly, vegetables form an important part of the Caribbean diet and are always served with main course dishes.

Stir-fried pak choi with almonds *(serves 4)*

1lb/450g pak choi, trimmed and shredded

2 tablespoons vegetable oil

6 spring onions, trimmed and finely sliced

1 garlic clove, crushed

soy sauce

1oz/25g flaked almonds, toasted

Heat the oil in a large pan or wok and gently fry the spring onions and garlic, then add the pak choi and continue cooking until just tender. Remove from the heat and add soy sauce to taste and the flaked almonds. Toss before serving.

Yam and onion cakes *(serves 4)*

1lb/450g yellow-fleshed yam, peeled and diced

8oz/225g onion, peeled and finely chopped

2 garlic cloves, crushed

¼ teaspoon ground allspice

dash of hot pepper sauce

black pepper

1 tablespoon vegetable oil

extra vegetable oil

Heat the tablespoonful of oil and fry the onion and garlic until soft. Boil the yam until tender, then drain and mash, add to the onion and garlic with the ground allspice and hot pepper sauce and season with black pepper, mixing thoroughly. Take rounded tablespoonfuls of the mixture and shape into flat rounds of about ¾ inch/2cm thick. Brush the cakes all over with oil and put them on a baking tray. Bake in a preheated oven at 180°C/350°F/Gas mark 4 for 25 minutes, turning once.

Baked pumpkin slices *(serves 4)*

1 small pumpkin

vegan margaine

black pepper

Cut the pumpkin into 8 wedges and remove the seeds and pith. Place the wedges on a greased baking tray and dot with margarine. Season with black pepper and bake in a preheated oven at 180°C/350°F/Gas mark 4 for about 40 minutes until tender.

Grilled vegetables *(serves 6)*

2lb/900g prepared vegetables (e.g. peppers, aubergine, courgette, mushrooms, onion), cut into equal-sized pieces

sprigs of fresh thyme

marinade

8 spring onions, trimmed and chopped

3 garlic cloves, chopped

1 inch/2.5cm piece of root ginger, chopped

2 tablespoons sunflower oil

1 tablespoon tamarind purée

1 dessertspoon lime juice

1 dessertspoon demerara sugar

¼ teaspoon ground allspice

pinch of chilli powder

black pepper

Blend all the marinade ingredients until smooth. Put the vegetables in a large bowl and mix in the marinade until they are coated. Cover and refrigerate for 2 hours. Transfer the vegetables to an ovenproof tray and place under a moderate grill until tender, turning frequently to ensure even cooking. Alternatively, the vegetables can be threaded onto skewers and cooked as kebabs, either under the grill or on a barbecue. Garnish with sprigs of fresh thyme.

Pumpkin and potato purée *(serves 4)*

1lb/450g pumpkin flesh, diced

1lb/450g potatoes, peeled and diced

1 rounded tablespoon vegan margarine

dash of hot pepper sauce

¼ teaspoon ground mace

black pepper

Steam the pumpkin, then mash until smooth. Boil the potatoes, drain and dry off over a low heat. Mash the potato with the margarine, then add to the pumpkin together with the pepper sauce and ground mace. Season with black pepper and mix thoroughly. Spoon into an ovenproof dish and cover with foil. Place in a preheated oven at 180°C/350°F/Gas mark 4 for about 15 minutes until heated through.

Baked sweet potato wedges

8-10oz/225-300g sweet potato per person

olive oil

hot pepper sauce

black pepper

Peel the potatoes thinly and cut them into wedge shapes. Mix a little hot pepper sauce with olive oil and brush this all over the potato wedges. Put them in a baking tin and season with black pepper. Cover with foil and bake in a preheated oven at 200°C/400°F/Gas mark 6 for about an hour until done. Turn several times to ensure even cooking.

Yam and sweet potato slices in coconut and ginger sauce *(serves 4)*

1lb/450g yam, peeled and sliced

1lb/450g sweet potato, peeled and sliced

6 spring onions, trimmed and sliced

7 fl.oz/200ml thick coconut milk

3 fl.oz/75ml vegetable stock

1 inch/2.5cm piece of root ginger, peeled and grated

1 dessertspoon vegetable oil

chopped fresh parsley

Heat the oil and gently fry the ginger and the white parts of the spring onions until softened. Remove from the heat and stir in the coconut milk and stock. Mix well.

Bring a large pan of water to the boil, add the yam and sweet potato slices and simmer for 3 minutes. Drain and carefully stir the slices into the sauce. Transfer to a greased shallow baking dish and cover with foil. Bake in a preheated oven at 180°C/350°F/Gas mark 4 for about 35 minutes until tender. Garnish with the green parts of the spring onions and finely chopped fresh parsley.

Spiced okra *(serves 4)*

12oz/350g okra, topped and tailed

8oz/225g tomatoes, skinned and chopped

1 onion, peeled and finely chopped

1 stick of celery, trimmed and finely sliced

2 garlic cloves, crushed

1 tablespoon vegetable oil

6 fl.oz/175ml vegetable stock

2 rounded teaspoons ground coriander

1 teaspoon ground cumin

½ teaspoon turmeric

¼ teaspoon chilli powder

black pepper

chopped fresh coriander leaves

Gently fry the onion, celery and garlic in the oil until soft. Add the coriander, cumin, turmeric and chilli powder and stir around for 1 minute. Add the tomatoes and cook until pulpy. Cut the okra into diagonal slices and add, together with the vegetable stock. Season with black pepper and stir well. Simmer until the okra is cooked, stirring frequently to prevent sticking. Put into a warmed serving dish and garnish with chopped fresh coriander leaves.

Split pea pudding *(serves 4/6)*

1lb/450g split peas

1 large onion, peeled and chopped

2oz/50g vegan margarine

4 tablespoons soya milk

1 bay leaf

1 teaspoon mixed herbs

black pepper

Soak the split peas in water overnight. Drain and rinse and put in a fresh pan of water with the onion and bay leaf. Bring to the boil, cover and simmer briskly until the peas are soft. Drain and remove the bay leaf. Rub the peas and onion through a sieve or mash or blend until smooth. Stir in the margarine, soya milk and mixed herbs and season with black pepper. Mix well, then spoon into a greased ovenproof dish and bake in a preheated oven at 180°C/350°F/Gas mark 4 for about 30 minutes until browned.

Vegetable trio *(serves 4)*

8oz/225g green beans, topped, tailed and cut into 1 inch/2.5cm lengths

8oz/225g carrot, scraped, cut in half lengthwise and finely sliced

4oz/100g green cabbage, finely shredded

2 garlic cloves, crushed

1oz/25g vegan margarine

4 tablespoons water

1 tablespoon lime juice

1 dessertspoon hot pepper sauce

1 dessertspoon chopped fresh parsley

black pepper

Melt the margarine in a large pan and add the vegetables and remaining ingredients. Stir well and cook over a medium heat for 10-15 minutes until the vegetables are tender. Stir frequently to prevent sticking.

Baked eddo with coconut *(serves 4)*

1½lb/675g eddo, peeled and diced

12 fl.oz/350ml vegetable stock

1oz/25g creamed coconut, grated

1 onion, peeled and finely chopped

1 dessertspoon vegetable oil

1 rounded teaspoon demerara sugar

½ teaspoon turmeric

pinch of cayenne pepper

black pepper

toasted flaked coconut

Heat the oil and gently fry the onion until softened. Dissolve the creamed coconut in the vegetable stock and add to the pan together with the remaining ingredients, except the flaked coconut, and stir well. Bring to the boil and simmer for 10 minutes, stirring frequently. Transfer to a casserole dish, cover with foil and bake in a preheated oven at 180°C/350°F/Gas mark 4 for 30-35 minutes until cooked. Garnish with the toasted flaked coconut.

Spiced jingy with red beans and ackee *(serves 6)*

1lb/450g jingy or courgette, sliced

8oz/225g cooked red kidney beans

8oz/225g drained and rinsed ackee

8oz/225g tomatoes, skinned and chopped

1 onion, peeled and chopped

2 garlic cloves

1 small red chilli, finely chopped

1 tablespoon vegetable oil

1 rounded teaspoon ground coriander

1 teaspoon ground cumin

black pepper

4 fl.oz/125ml vegetable stock

chopped fresh coriander leaves

Fry the onion, garlic and chilli in the oil in a large pan until soft. Add the ground coriander and cumin and stir around for 1 minute, then the tomatoes and cook until pulpy. Stir in the jingy or courgette and stock and season with black pepper. Bring to the boil, cover and simmer for about 20 minutes until the vegetables are just done. Stir frequently to prevent sticking. Add the red kidney beans and carefully stir in the ackee. Cook for a couple of minutes until heated through, put in a warmed serving dish and garnish with chopped fresh coriander.

SALADS

Potato salads and coleslaw are particular favourites all over the Caribbean, with different regions having their own ways of preparing them. Some prefer their coleslaw made with white cabbage, some prefer red, while in other areas it is made with a mixture of the two. Avocados are used in lots of salad recipes and these combine particularly well with tomatoes and Caribbean seasonings.

Tomato, avocado and cucumber salad *(serves 4)*

8oz/225g tomatoes, chopped

1 large, ripe avocado, peeled, stoned and diced

4oz/100g cucumber, chopped

4 spring onions, trimmed and sliced

1 dessertspoon lime juice

1 dessertspoon olive oil

1 tablespoon light malt vinegar

dash of hot pepper sauce

black pepper

1 tablespoon finely chopped fresh parsley

shredded lettuce leaves

Combine the tomatoes, avocado, cucumber, spring onions and parsley in a large bowl. Mix the lime juice with the olive oil, vinegar and hot pepper sauce. Season with black pepper and spoon the dressing over the salad. Toss well. Arrange some shredded lettuce leaves on a serving plate and pile the salad on top.

Mixed green salad *(serves 6)*

½ small crisp lettuce, chopped

1 bunch of watercress, trimmed

¼ cucumber, chopped

1 green pepper, sliced

1 stick of celery, trimmed and sliced

6 spring onions, trimmed and sliced

1 large ripe avocado, peeled and diced

1 garlic clove, crushed

2 tablespoons olive oil

1 tablespoon white wine vinegar

1 dessertspoon lime juice

lemon juice

black pepper

chopped fresh parsley and chives

Sprinkle the avocado with lemon juice and put it in a serving bowl with the lettuce, watercress, cucumber, green pepper, celery and spring onions. Mix the olive oil with the white wine vinegar, lime juice and garlic, season with black pepper and spoon over the salad. Toss well and garnish with chopped fresh parsley and chives.

Potato and tomato salad *(serves 4)*

2lb/900g potatoes, peeled and diced

chopped fresh coriander

dressing

8oz/225g ripe tomatoes, skinned and chopped

1 small onion, peeled and grated

2 garlic cloves, crushed

¼oz/7g creamed coconut, grated

1 dessertspoon vegetable oil

1 dessertspoon tamarind purée

¼ teaspoon paprika

black pepper

Heat the oil and gently fry the onion and garlic until soft. Add the remaining dressing ingredients and stir well. Bring to the boil, cover and simmer gently until the mixture reduces down and thickens.

Boil the potatoes until tender, drain and add to the dressing. Toss well and transfer the salad to a serving bowl. Cover and refrigerate until cold. Garnish with chopped fresh coriander leaves when serving.

Nutty bean salad *(serves 4)*

8oz/225g mixed cooked beans (e.g. black-eye, red kidney, chickpeas, gungo peas)

4oz/100g green beans, cut into ½ inch/1cm lengths

4oz/100g tomato, skinned and chopped

1 small red onion, peeled and finely chopped

1 garlic clove, crushed

few slices of Scotch bonnet pepper

1oz/25g cashew nuts, halved and toasted

1 dessertspoon olive oil

1 teaspoon thyme

black pepper

shredded lettuce leaves

Steam the green beans until just done and rinse them under cold water. Gently fry the onion and garlic in the oil until softened. Remove from the heat and add the steamed beans, tomato, Scotch bonnet pepper and thyme. Season with black pepper and mix very well. Transfer to a lidded container and chill. Arrange the shredded lettuce on a serving plate. Stir the cashew nuts into the bean salad and pile it on the lettuce.

Christophene salad *(serves 4)*

1 large or 2 small christophenes, peeled, stoned and diced

4oz/100g mushrooms, wiped and chopped

4oz/100g sweetcorn kernels

4 spring onions, trimmed and sliced

1 tomato, chopped

chopped fresh chives

dressing

1 tablespoon olive oil

1 dessertspoon white wine vinegar

1 teaspoon lemon juice

½ teaspoon thyme

1 garlic clove, crushed

black pepper

Blanch the christophene and sweetcorn in boiling water for 1 minute, then drain and rinse under cold water. Drain well and put in a mixing bowl with the mushrooms, spring onions and tomato. Mix the dressing ingredients together and spoon over the salad. Toss well and transfer the salad to a serving bowl. Garnish with chopped fresh chives and chill.

Coleslaw *(serves 4)*

4oz/100g white cabbage, finely shredded

4oz/100g red cabbage, finely shredded

2oz/50g carrot, scraped and grated

2oz/50g red pepper, finely sliced

1 celery stick, trimmed and finely sliced

4 spring onions, trimmed and finely chopped

2 tablespoons olive oil

1 dessertspoon soy sauce

1 dessertpoon finely chopped fresh parsley

1 teaspoon lemon juice

black pepper

Combine the white and red cabbage, carrot, pepper, celery, spring onions and parsley in a large bowl. Mix the olive oil with the soy sauce and lemon juice and pour over the salad. Season with black pepper and toss thoroughly. Transfer to a serving bowl, cover and chill before serving.

Avocado and pepper salad *(serves 4)*

2 ripe avocados, peeled, stoned and diced

6oz/175g red pepper, chopped

6oz/175g yellow pepper, chopped

2oz/50g mushrooms, wiped and sliced

1 red onion, peeled and finely chopped

½ small green chilli, finely chopped

2 garlic cloves, crushed

1 tablespoon olive oil

½ teaspoon thyme

1 teaspoon parsley

1 teaspoon lime juice

1 teaspoon soy sauce

black pepper

chopped fresh parsley

Stir fry the red and yellow peppers, mushrooms, onion, chilli and garlic in the olive oil for 2 minutes. Remove from the heat and add the remaining ingredients apart from the avocado and fresh parsley. Stir well and refrigerate until cold. Add the avocado, mix well and spoon into a serving bowl. Serve garnished with chopped fresh parsley.

Sweet potato and chickpea salad *(serves 4/6)*

1lb/450g sweet potato, peeled and diced

8oz/225g cooked chickpeas

4oz/100g red pepper, finely chopped

4 spring onions, trimmed and finely sliced

chopped fresh parsley

dressing

1 tablespoon olive oil

1 tablespoon white wine vinegar

1 teaspoon soy sauce

½ teaspoon paprika

black pepper

Steam the potatoes until tender. Put them in a lidded container and refrigerate until cold, then mix in the chickpeas, red pepper and spring onions. Mix the dressing ingredients until well combined, spoon over the salad and toss. Transfer to a serving bowl, cover and chill. Garnish with chopped fresh parsley.

CHUTNEYS, SALSAS AND SAUCES

The produce that grows in abundance on the islands is admirably suited to making chutneys, which were first introduced by the East Indian immigrants. Chutneys made from fresh fruits and spices go especially well with rice and curried dishes. Evidence of the Central American influence on the cuisine is provided by the recipes for salsas. Savoury little uncooked relishes made from fruits and vegetables, they are served with appetisers, salads, rice, pies and vegetables. Sauces with a Caribbean flavour give an authentic taste to plain cooked rice or steamed vegetables.

Mango and ginger chutney
(makes approx. 3lb/1.5kg)

2lb/900g firm mango, peeled and chopped

3oz/75g stem ginger, finely chopped

8oz/225g onion, peeled and finely chopped

4oz/100g sultanas, chopped

3oz/75g demerara sugar

8 fl.oz/225ml light malt vinegar

¼ teaspoon ground allspice

¼ teaspoon ground cinnamon

¼ teaspoon cayenne pepper

Put all the ingredients in a large saucepan and stir. Bring to the boil, then simmer uncovered for about 35 minutes until the mixture reduces and thickens. Stir frequently to prevent sticking. Spoon into warm, sterilised jars and cover.

Pineapple, apple and raisin chutney
(makes approx. 3$\frac{1}{2}$lb/1.6kg)

1 pineapple of approx. 2½lb/1.1kg, peeled and finely chopped

1lb/450g cooking apples, peeled, cored and finely chopped

8oz/225g onion, peeled and finely chopped

4oz/100g raisins

4oz/100g soft brown sugar

8 fl.oz/225ml light malt vinegar

½ teaspoon ground coriander

¼ teaspoon ground allspice

¼ teaspoon ground cloves

Put all the ingredients into a large saucepan, stir and bring to the boil. Simmer uncovered for about 35-40 minutes until the chutney is reduced and thickens, stirring frequently. Spoon into warm, sterilised jars and cover.

Banana, date and coconut chutney
(makes approx. 3lb/1.5kg)

1½lb/675g firm bananas, peeled and chopped

8oz/225g stoned dates, chopped

2oz/50g demerara sugar

1oz/25g stem ginger, finely chopped

1oz/25g creamed coconut, grated

15 fl.oz/450ml white wine vinegar

¼ teaspoon ground allspice

¼ teaspoon ground cloves

Bring the dates and vinegar to the boil in a large pan. Cover and simmer gently for 3 minutes, then remove from the heat and add the remaining ingredients. Stir well and bring back to the boil. Lower the heat and cook for about 10 minutes, whilst stirring, until the bananas soften and the mixture reduces and thickens. Spoon into warm, sterilised jars and cover.

Red onion and tomato salsa *(serves 4/6)*

8oz/225g red onion, peeled and finely chopped

8oz/225g ripe tomatoes, skinned and finely chopped

1 small red chilli, finely chopped

1 garlic clove, crushed

1 tablespoon white wine vinegar

1 dessertspoon demerara sugar

dash of soy sauce

¼ teaspoon paprika

black pepper

Combine all the ingredients and refrigerate.

Mango salsa *(serves 4/6)*

1 large mango, peeled and finely chopped

4 spring onions, trimmed and finely chopped

1 garlic clove, crushed

1 small green chilli, finely chopped

1 tablespoon lime juice

2 tablespoons finely chopped fresh coriander

Mix all the ingredients together and chill before serving.

Paw paw and pepper salsa *(serves 4/6)*

1 paw paw

2oz/50g red pepper, finely chopped

2oz/50g green pepper, finely chopped

2oz/50g yellow pepper, finely chopped

1 stick of celery, trimmed and finely chopped

1 small red onion, peeled and finely chopped

1 teaspoon soy sauce

1 dessertspoon lime juice

Peel the paw paw and remove the seeds. Chop the flesh finely and mix it with the other ingredients. Chill before serving.

Coconut sauce *(serves 4)*

1oz/25g creamed coconut

10 fl.oz/300ml vegetable stock

1 garlic clove, crushed

1 teaspoon vegetable oil

2 rounded dessertspoons cornflour

Heat the oil and gently fry the garlic, then add the coconut and stir until dissolved. Mix the cornflour with the stock until smooth and add to the pan. Stir well and bring to the boil whilst stirring. Continue stirring for a minute or two until the sauce thickens.

Peanut and pepper sauce *(serves 4)*

2 rounded tablespoons smooth peanut butter

1 dessertspoon groundnut or vegetable oil

2 garlic cloves, crushed

10 fl.oz/300ml vegetable stock

1 dessertspoon soy sauce

hot pepper sauce to taste

2 rounded dessertspoons cornflour

Gently fry the garlic in the oil. Remove from the heat and add the peanut butter, soy sauce and hot pepper sauce. Dissolve the cornflour in the vegetable stock and add. Stir well and return to the heat. Bring to the boil whilst stirring and continue stirring for a couple of minutes until the sauce thickens.

Tomato and tamarind sauce *(serves 4)*

12oz/350g ripe tomatoes, skinned and chopped

2 garlic cloves, crushed

3 fl.oz/75ml water

1 dessertspoon vegetable oil

1 dessertspoon tomato purée

1 tablespoon tamarind purée

black pepper

Fry the garlic in the oil, add the remaining ingredients and stir well. Bring to the boil, cover and simmer until the tomatoes become pulpy. Remove from the heat and mash with the back of a spoon or a potato masher. Return to the heat and cook gently for a few minutes until the sauce thickens, stirring frequently to prevent sticking.

DESSERTS

Many of the desserts will be recognised from other cuisines, but the ones included here have a distinctive Caribbean flavour. Home-made ice creams and sorbets are very popular and can easily be made from almost any fruit. Fresh fruit salads are given the Caribbean touch by adding stem ginger, rum and lime juice and garnishing with flaked coconut. Fruit pies and tarts are also favourites, especially those made with pineapple and a variety of cherry that grows wild on some of the islands.

As well as the numerous and varied fruits, some vegetables are also put to good use in dessert making. Steamed sweet potato and fruit pudding is a kind of lighter version of Christmas pudding, while yam combines perfectly with coconut in yam and coconut bread pudding to give this familiar dessert a Caribbean feel. The type of pumpkin most popular in the region is a thin-skinned green variety called calabaza, although other varieties work equally well for sweet and savoury dishes.

Paw paw with mango fool *(serves 4)*

2 ripe paw paws, peeled and diced

toasted flaked almonds

mango fool

1 small nearly ripe mango, peeled and diced

5 fl.oz/150ml tropical fruit juice

1 teaspoon lime juice

1 rounded tablespoon demerara sugar

5 fl.oz/150ml soya milk

1 teaspoon vanilla essence

1 rounded tablespoon cornflour

Divide the paw paw between 4 dishes. Put the mango, fruit juice, lime juice and sugar in a saucepan and bring to the boil, cover and simmer gently for about 10 minutes until the mango is soft. Allow to cool slightly, then put the mango and remaining juice in a liquidiser and blend until smooth. Dissolve the cornflour and vanilla essence in the soya milk and add to the mango purée. Mix together thoroughly then heat gently, whilst stirring, to boiling point. Spoon the fool over the paw paw and cover and chill for a few hours until set. Garnish with toasted flaked almonds when serving.

Grapefruit and guava cocktail *(serves 4)*

14oz/400g tin guavas in syrup

1 grapefruit

fresh grapefruit juice

demerara sugar

1 teaspoon agar agar

Peel the grapefruit and remove all the pith and membranes. Chop the segments and strain the juice into a measuring jug. Sweeten the segments with a little demerara sugar. Strain the guava syrup into the measuring jug and make up to 10 fl.oz/300ml with fresh grapefruit juice. Add the agar agar and stir until dissolved. Cut one of the guava halves into 4 slices and keep for garnish. Chop the remaining guava and add to the chopped grapefruit, mix well and divide between 4 serving dishes. Heat the grapefruit and guava syrup gently to just below boiling point in a small saucepan. Pour over the fruit in the dishes, cover and put in the fridge for a few hours until set. Garnish each dish with a slice of guava.

Tropical fruits with mango ice *(serves 6)*

mango ice

1 medium-sized ripe mango, peeled and diced

2 tablespoons lemon juice

8 fl.oz/225ml plain soya yoghurt

1oz/25g soft brown sugar

fruit salad

2lb/900g tropical fruit (i.e. a selection of paw paw, pineapple, passion fruit, melon, starfruit, banana, guava)

2 pieces stem ginger, finely chopped

4 fl.oz/125ml tropical fruit juice

2 tablespoons dark rum

toasted flaked coconut

Put the ingredients for the mango ice in a blender and blend until smooth. Pour into a shallow freezerproof container, cover and freeze for 2 hours. Remove from the freezer and whisk, then return to the freezer until just frozen. (Keep at room temperature for 30 minutes before serving if the ice becomes too hard.)

Prepare the fruit by peeling and dicing or slicing into evenly-sized pieces and put them in a serving bowl with the ginger. Mix the fruit juice with the rum and pour over the fruit. Stir well, cover and chill for a couple of hours. Serve the mango ice with the fruit, garnished with toasted flaked coconut.

Pineapple and coconut brulée *(serves 4)*

1lb/450g pineapple, finely chopped

6 fl.oz/175ml water

½oz/15g creamed coconut

8 fl.oz/225ml soya milk

1oz/25g cornflour

1 rounded tablespoon demerara sugar
1 teaspoon vanilla essence
extra demerara sugar
toasted flaked coconut

Drain half of the chopped pineapple and divide between 4 3¹/₂ inch/9cm ramekin dishes. Put the remaining pineapple in a saucepan with the creamed coconut and water, bring to the boil, cover and simmer for 5 minutes. Allow to cool, then blend until smooth. Pass through a fine sieve, pressing it through with the back of a spoon, into a double boiler. Dissolve the cornflour, rounded tablespoonful of sugar and vanilla essence in the soya milk and add to the pan. Stir well, bring to the boil whilst stirring and continue stirring until the custard thickens. Pour the custard over the pineapple in the ramekin dishes. Cover and refrigerate for a few hours until set. Sprinkle the tops with demerara sugar and place under a hot grill for a minute or two until the sugar dissolves. Return to the fridge to cool. Garnish with toasted flaked coconut when serving.

Coconut and rum ice *(serves 6)*

14 fl.oz/400ml tin of coconut milk
6 fl.oz/175ml plain soya yoghurt
1oz/25g granulated sugar
3 tablespoons dark rum

Put all the ingredients in a bowl and whisk until smooth. Pour into a shallow, freezerproof container and cover. Freeze for 2 hours, then remove from the freezer and whisk again. Return to the freezer until just frozen. Keep at room temperature for 30 minutes before serving if the ice has become too hard.

Orange and almond pudding *(serves 6)*

4oz/100g fine wholemeal self raising flour

4oz/100g cornmeal

3oz/75g vegan margarine

2oz/50g demerara sugar

2oz/50g ground almonds

1oz/25g flaked almonds, chopped

finely grated peel of 1 orange

5 fl.oz/150ml fresh orange juice

1 rounded tablespoon golden syrup

1 rounded tablespoon orange marmalade

toasted flaked almonds

Put the margarine, sugar and golden syrup in a large saucepan and heat gently until melted. Remove from the heat and stir in the orange peel, cornmeal, ground and chopped almonds. Gradually mix in the flour and orange juice, then spoon the mixture into a lined and greased 7 inch/18cm diameter flan tin and level the top. Bake in a preheated oven at 180°C/350°F/Gas mark 4 for 30 minutes until golden. Gently heat the marmalade in a small saucepan until runny. Spread it evenly over the top of the pudding and sprinkle with the toasted flaked almonds. Cut into wedges and serve hot with vegan ice cream.

Pumpkin and almond pie *(serves 6)*

pastry

5oz/150g fine wholemeal self raising flour

1oz/25g ground almonds

2½oz/65g vegan margarine

½ teaspoon almond essence

water

filling

1¼lb/550g pumpkin

2 fl.oz/50ml fresh orange juice

3oz/75g ground almonds

2oz/50g demerara sugar

2oz/50g fine wholemeal self raising flour

½ teaspoon ground cinnamon

¼ teaspoon grated nutmeg

½oz/15g flaked almonds

Mix the ground almonds with the flour and rub in the margarine. Add the almond essence and enough water to bind. Turn out onto a floured board and roll out to line a greased 8 inch/20cm diameter loose-bottomed flan tin. Prick the base and bake blind in a preheated oven at 180°C/350°F/Gas mark 4 for 5 minutes.

Peel the pumpkin and discard the pulpy centre and seeds. Grate the flesh and put it into a saucepan with the orange juice. Bring to the boil and cook for 3 minutes whilst stirring, then remove from the heat and add the remaining filling ingredients apart from the flaked almonds, mixing well. Spoon the filling evenly into the pastry flan case. Sprinkle the flaked almonds on top and press them in lightly with the back of a spoon. Return the pie to the oven and bake for 30-35 minutes until golden brown. Carefully remove from the tin, cut into wedges and serve hot.

Steamed sweet potato and fruit pudding (*serves 4/6*)

8oz/225g sweet potato, peeled

4oz/100g mixed cake fruit

4oz/100g dried dates, finely chopped

4oz/100g fine wholemeal self raising flour

2oz/50g breadcrumbs

2oz/50g vegan margarine

1oz/25g demerara sugar

½oz/15g soya flour

2 tablespoons dark rum or orange juice

1 tablespoon molasses

1 teaspoon ground allspice

Cut the sweet potato into even-sized chunks and boil them for 3 minutes. Drain and when cooled grate the chunks.

Cream the margarine with the sugar and molasses in a large bowl. Whisk the soya flour with the rum or orange juice, add to the bowl and beat until smooth. Stir in the mixed cake fruit and dates, then the grated potato and the breadcrumbs. Add the sifted flour and ground allspice and combine thoroughly. Spoon the mixture into a greased $1^{1}/_{2}$ pint/900ml pudding bowl, pressing it down firmly and evenly with the back of a spoon. Cover with a double layer of greaseproof paper and a layer of foil and tie the top on securely. Put the pudding bowl in a saucepan and fill it with water to three-quarters of the height of the bowl. Bring to the boil, cover and simmer for 1 hour. Keep the water topped up to the three-quarter mark and make sure it simmers briskly. Remove the covering and run a sharp knife around the pudding, then invert it onto a serving plate. Cut into wedges and serve hot with vegan ice cream or yoghurt.

Paw paw and lime sorbet *(serves 6)*

2 paw paws

10 fl.oz/300ml water

2oz/50g granulated sugar

2 tablespoons lime juice

Peel the paw paws and discard the seeds. Chop the flesh and put it in a saucepan with the other ingredients. Stir well and bring to the boil. Simmer gently for 2 minutes, then allow to cool slightly and liquidise until smooth. Pour into a shallow freezerproof tray, cover and freeze for 2 hours. Whisk the sorbet to break up the ice crystals and return to the freezer until just frozen. If frozen too hard, keep at room temperature for 30 minutes before serving.

Ginger and orange trifles *(serves 6)*

8oz/225g ginger cake (see page 98), chopped

2 oranges

2 pieces of stem ginger, chopped

12 fl.oz/350ml fresh orange juice

1 teaspoon agar agar

16 fl.oz/475ml soya milk

2 rounded tablespoons demerara sugar

2 rounded tablespoons custard powder

½ teaspoon ground ginger

Divide the ginger cake between 6 sundae dishes. Peel one of the oranges and remove all the pith and membranes. Chop the segments and mix with the stem ginger. Spoon on top of the cake in the dishes. Dissolve the agar agar in the orange juice and heat gently whilst stirring to just below boiling point. Pour over the cake and fruit in the dishes, cover and chill until set.

Mix the custard powder, sugar and ground ginger with a little of the soya milk until smooth. Bring the remaining soya milk to the boil and stir into the custard mixture. Transfer to a double boiler and bring to the boil whilst stirring, continuing to stir until the custard thickens. Pour over the jelly in the dishes. Cover and refrigerate for a few hours. Peel the remaining orange and remove all pith. Cut the orange into thin slices and use these to garnish the trifles.

Banana and pineapple pancakes *(serves 4)*

pancakes

4oz/100g plain flour

1oz/25g soya flour

12 fl.oz/350ml soya milk

1 rounded teaspoon ground cinnamon

vegan margarine

filling

1½lb/675g fresh pineapple, peeled and chopped

1lb/450g bananas, peeled and sliced

1oz/25g sultanas

4 tablespoons tropical fruit juice

1 tablespoon demerara sugar

¼ teaspoon ground allspice

to serve

lime juice

demerara sugar

Whisk the flours and cinnamon with the soya milk until smooth. Cover and chill for 2 hours. Whisk again, then melt some margarine in an 8 inch/20cm diameter frying pan and make 8 pancakes. Keep them warm while making the filling.

Put all the filling ingredients in a saucepan and heat gently whilst stirring until the banana begins to soften. Divide the filling between the pancakes and fold them over to enclose. Sprinkle the tops with lime juice and demerara sugar.

Yam and coconut bread pudding *(serves 6)*

8oz/225g yam, peeled and diced

6oz/175g mixed cake fruit

4oz/100g breadcrumbs

2oz/50g desiccated coconut

2oz/50g vegan margarine

2oz/50g demerara sugar

1 rounded tablespoon golden syrup

1 rounded teaspoon ground allspice

4 fl.oz/125ml tropical fruit juice

1 rounded tablespoon soya flour

extra desiccated coconut

Boil the yam, drain and mash until smooth. Cream the margarine with the sugar and golden syrup in a mixing bowl. Whisk the soya flour with the fruit juice and add to the bowl together with the coconut, allspice and mixed fruit. Add the mashed yam and breadcrumbs and combine well. Spoon the mixture into a lined and greased 9 x 6 inch/23 x 15cm baking tin. Press down firmly and evenly. Sprinkle the top with desiccated coconut and lightly press this in with the back of a spoon. Bake in a preheated oven at 180°C/350°F/Gas mark 4 for about 30 minutes until browned. Serve hot with vegan ice cream or yoghurt.

BAKING

U sed in all manner of dishes, coconut adds a creamy, nutty richness and gives a wonderful aroma when cooking, especially in baking recipes. Jamaican ginger is reputed to be the best in the world and Jamaican ginger cake is renowned. Jamaica is also famed for its coffee, which is grown in the Blue Mountain area. It is the rarest and most expensive and it is exported to all corners of the globe. Sponge and gateau-type cakes are very popular and many believe that these were first introduced by the British. Rich fruit cakes are also favourites and usually contain copious amounts of alcohol. Other ingredients that are essential in baking recipes and help give that authentic Caribbean flavour are the many spices that are grown in the region.

Coconut and currant bread

12oz/350g plain white flour

4oz/100g currants

2oz/50g creamed coconut, grated

2oz/50g vegan margarine, melted

1oz/25g demerara sugar

5 fl.oz/150ml hot water

1 teaspoon ground allspice

2 teaspoons easy-blend yeast

soya milk

Combine the flour, sugar, ground allspice and yeast in a large bowl and stir in the currants and melted margarine. Mix the creamed coconut with the hot water until it dissolves. Add this to the bowl and stir thoroughly until a soft dough forms. Turn it out onto a floured board and knead well. Return it to the bowl, cover and leave in a warm place for 1 hour until well risen. Knead the dough again, then put it in an 8 inch/20cm greased loaf tin, pressing it gently into the corners to fill. Cover and leave in a warm place for 30 minutes to rise. Brush the top with soya milk and bake in a preheated oven at 180°C/350°F/Gas mark 4 for about 30 minutes until golden brown. Turn out onto a wire rack to cool. Serve cut into slices.

Chocolate, rum and raisin cake

8oz/225g fine wholemeal self raising flour

6oz/175g raisins, chopped

3oz/75g vegan margarine

2oz/50g demerara sugar

1 tablespoon molasses

1 tablespoon cocoa powder

2 tablespoons dark rum

1 teaspoon ground cinnamon

7 fl.oz/200ml soya milk

topping

2oz/50g vegan chocolate, broken

toasted flaked coconut

Put the raisins and rum in a lidded container and leave to soak for 1 hour. Gently heat the margarine, sugar and molasses in a large saucepan until melted. Remove from the heat and stir in the raisins and any remaining rum. Add the sifted flour, cocoa powder and cinnamon and then the soya milk. Mix thoroughly, then spoon the mixture into a lined and greased 7 inch/18cm diameter baking tin. Level the top and bake in a preheated oven at 180°C/350°F/Gas mark 4 for about 25 minutes until risen and firm in the centre. Turn out onto a wire rack to cool.

Melt the chocolate in a bowl over a pan of boiling water. Spread it evenly over the top and sides of the cake and sprinkle the top with toasted flaked coconut. Keep in the fridge until the chocolate sets. Cut into wedges to serve.

Spiced pumpkin bun

12oz/350g pumpkin

12oz/350g fine wholemeal self raising flour

8oz/225g sultanas

3oz/75g demerara sugar

4 fl.oz/125ml sunflower oil

5 fl.oz/150ml strong black tea

1 rounded dessertspoon molasses

1 teaspoon ground allspice

½ teaspoon ground mace

Put the sultanas and tea in a mixing bowl to soak for 30 minutes, then stir in the sunflower oil, sugar and molasses. Peel the pumpkin and discard the pulpy centre and seeds. Grate the flesh and add it to the bowl together with the sifted flour and spices. Combine everything well, then spoon the mixture evenly into a base-lined and greased 10 inch/25cm loaf tin. Press down firmly and cover with foil. Bake in a preheated oven at 180°C/350°F/Gas mark 4 for 1 hour, remove the foil and bake for 10-15 minutes more until a skewer comes out clean when inserted in the centre. Leave in the tin for 10 minutes, then run a sharp knife around the edges and turn the bun out onto a wire rack to cool completely. Serve cut into slices.

Pineapple and coconut buns *(makes 9)*

6oz/175g fine wholemeal self raising flour

4oz/100g fresh pineapple, chopped

2oz/50g vegan margarine

2oz/50g demerara sugar

2oz/50g raisins, chopped

1½oz/40g desiccated coconut

¼ teaspoon ground allspice

4 fl.oz/125ml pineapple juice

extra desiccated coconut

Blend the pineapple and pineapple juice. Melt the margarine and sugar over a low heat in a large saucepan. Remove from the heat and add the pineapple, coconut, raisins and allspice, then stir in the flour and mix thoroughly. Divide the mixture between 9 greased holes of a bun tin (or use paper cake cases). Sprinkle the tops with desiccated coconut and bake in a preheated oven at 180°C/350°F/Gas mark 4 for about 20 minutes until golden. Carefully turn the buns out onto a wire rack to get cold.

Ginger cake *(serves 8)*

6oz/175g fine wholemeal self raising flour

2oz/50g vegan margarine

2oz/50g demerara sugar

2oz/50g sultanas, chopped

1oz/25g stem ginger, finely chopped

1oz/25g stem ginger, finely sliced

1oz/25g soya flour

2 tablespoons dark rum or orange juice

2 tablespoons ginger syrup from stem ginger jar

1 rounded tablespoon molasses

1 rounded teaspoon ground ginger
4 fl.oz/125ml soya milk

Put the sultanas and chopped ginger in a bowl and add the rum or orange juice. Stir well, cover and leave for 1 hour. Heat the margarine, sugar, ginger syrup, molasses and ground ginger in a large saucepan until melted and well combined. Remove from the heat and stir in the soaked fruit with any remaining liquid and the soya flour. Gradually add the flour and the soya milk and mix thoroughly. Spoon the mixture into a lined and greased 7 inch/18cm square baking tin and level the top. Arrange the ginger slices on top and press in lightly. Bake in a preheated oven at 180°C/350°F/Gas mark 4 for about 25 minutes until golden brown. Carefully turn the cake out onto a wire rack to cool before cutting into 8 equal portions.

Banana loaf

12oz/350g ripe bananas, peeled and mashed
8oz/225g fine wholemeal self raising flour
2oz/50g vegan margarine
2oz/50g demerara sugar
4 fl.oz/125ml soya milk
½ teaspoon ground cinnamon

Cream the margarine with the sugar, and mix in the mashed banana and cinnamon. Gradually add the flour and soya milk and stir until well combined. Spoon the mixture into a base-lined and greased 8 inch/20cm loaf tin. Level the top and cover loosely with foil. Bake in a preheated oven at 180°C/350°F/Gas mark 4 for 1 hour. Remove the foil and bake for a further 15 minutes until the loaf is browned and a skewer comes out clean when inserted in the centre. Run a sharp knife around the edges to loosen and turn out onto a wire rack. Cut into slices to serve.

Creole fruit cake

12oz/350g fine wholemeal self raising four

8oz/225g sultanas

8oz/225g raisins

8oz/225g currants

4oz/100g dried dates, finely chopped

4oz/100g cut mixed peel

4oz/100g vegan margarine

4oz/100g demerara sugar

4oz/100g mixed nuts, finely chopped

2oz/50g glacé cherries, washed, dried and chopped

1 ripe banana (approx. 6oz/175g), peeled and mashed

3 fl.oz/75ml dark rum

3 fl.oz/75ml brandy

3 fl.oz/75ml port or sherry

3 fl.oz/75ml tropical fruit juice

1 rounded tablespoon molasses

1 teaspoon ground cinnamon

1 teaspoon ground cloves

extra rum

topping (optional)

apricot jam glaze

glacé fruits

whole nuts

Put the sultanas, raisins, currants, dates, mixed peel and cherries in a large saucepan. Add the rum, brandy, port or sherry and cinnamon and cloves and mix well. Cover and leave to marinate for 48 hours. Stir a few times during marinating.

Add the fruit juice and molasses and heat gently whilst stirring. Simmer for 5 minutes, stirring frequently, then remove from the heat and stir in the nuts. Cream the margarine with the sugar in a large bowl. Add the banana and combine until smooth, then the fruit and nut mixture, and finally gradually add the flour until a stiff consistency is obtained. Spoon the mixture into a lined and greased 8 inch/20cm diameter deep cake tin, pressing it down firmly and evenly. Cover loosely with foil and bake in a preheated oven at 150°C/300°F/Gas mark 2 for 2¼ hours, until a skewer inserted in the centre comes out clean. Allow to cool in the tin for 30 minutes, then transfer to a wire rack to get cold. Brush the top and sides of the cake with rum and spread the top with apricot jam glaze. Arrange a selection of glacé fruits and nuts on top and brush them with apricot glaze.

Sweet potato and citrus cake

8oz/225g sweet potato, peeled and grated

8oz/225g cut mixed peel

8oz/225g fine wholemeal self raising flour

3oz/75g vegan margarine

2oz/50g cornmeal

2oz/50g demerara sugar

4 fl.oz/125ml fresh orange juice

1 rounded tablespoon marmalade

1 tablespoon lime juice

1 teaspoon ground mixed spice

Bring the sweet potato, orange and lime juice to the boil and simmer for 1 minute whilst stirring, then remove from the heat and allow to cool.

Cream the margarine with the sugar and marmalade in a large bowl. Stir in the sweet potato mixture, cut mixed peel and cornmeal. Gradually add the sifted flour and mixed spice and combine thoroughly. Spoon the mixture into a lined and greased 7 inch/18cm diameter cake tin. Level the top and cover loosely with foil. Bake in a preheated oven at 180°C/350°F/Gas mark 4 for 1 hour, then remove the foil and bake for about 15 minutes more until golden. Leave in the tin for 15 minutes, then carefully transfer to a wire rack.

Coconut tarts *(makes 12)*

pastry
4oz/100g fine wholemeal self raising flour

1½oz/40g vegan margarine

water

filling
4oz/100g desiccated coconut

2oz/50g fine wholemeal self raising flour

1 rounded tablespoon golden syrup

1oz/25g vegan margarine

½ teaspoon ground ginger

½ teaspoon grated nutmeg

4 tablespoons soya milk

Rub the margarine into the flour and add enough water to make a soft dough. Turn out onto a floured board and roll out thinly. Cut into 2¾ inch/7cm circles with a biscuit cutter. Re-roll and cut the dough until it is all used up. Line a 12-holed greased tart tin with the pastry circles.

Put the margarine and golden syrup in a saucepan and heat gently until melted. Remove from the heat and add the remaining filling ingredients. Mix thoroughly, then divide the mixture between the 12 pastry cases, neatening the filling with the back of a spoon. Bake in a preheated oven at 180°C/350°F/Gas mark 4 for 20-25 minutes until golden brown. Serve either warm or cold.

Coffee, date and brazil nut gateau

9oz/250g fine wholemeal self raising flour

3oz/75g vegan margarine

2oz/50g demerara sugar

2oz/50g brazil nuts, grated

1 rounded tablespoon golden syrup

1 tablespoon Tia Maria

8 fl.oz/225ml strong black coffee

1 rounded teaspoon ground cinnamon

filling

4oz/100g stoned dried dates, chopped

3 fl.oz/75ml fresh orange juice

topping

2oz/50g vegan chocolate, broken

1 teaspoon ground coffee

½oz/15g brazil nuts, flaked

Heat the margarine, sugar and golden syrup in a large saucepan until melted. Remove from the heat and stir in the grated brazil nuts, coffee and Tia Maria. Gradually add the sifted flour and cinnamon and mix very well. Divide the mixture between 2 lined and greased 7 inch/18cm diameter sandwich tins, spreading it out evenly. Bake in a preheated oven at 180°C/350°F/Gas mark 4 for about 20 minutes, until golden and firm in the centres. Carefully transfer to a wire rack to cool.

Put the dates and orange juice in a small saucepan and bring to the boil. Simmer until the juice has been absorbed and the dates are soft. Stir frequently to prevent sticking. Remove from the heat and mash with the back of a spoon until the mixture is thick. Allow to cool, then spread the mixture onto one of the sponges. Place the other sponge on the top.

Melt the chocolate in a bowl over a pan of boiling water, add the ground coffee and mix well. Spread the chocolate evenly over the top and sides of the cake and sprinkle the flaked brazil nuts on top. Put in the fridge until set and cut into wedges to serve.

DRINKS

Produced in the Caribbean since the 17th century, rum is still the nations' favourite drink and it finds its way into numerous punches and cocktails as well as various sweet and savoury dishes. Nowadays, rum is a major export from the Caribbean and many different types are distilled, from white, golden and dark to special varieties flavoured with banana, coconut or pineapple. Ginger beer is another drink that is synonymous with the area and this is enjoyed either on its own or as a mixer. Juices from the plentiful supply of citrus fruits grown on the islands blend perfectly with other fruits and ingredients to create long, refreshing and thirst-quenching drinks.

Fruity rum punch *(serves 6)*

9 fl.oz/250ml dark rum

18 fl.oz/550ml ginger beer

27 fl.oz/800ml tropical fruit juice

crushed ice

Mix the rum with the ginger beer and tropical fruit juice. Pour into tumblers and add crushed ice.

Pineapple and guava malibu *(serves 4)*

1lb/450g tin pineapple rings in natural juice

10 fl.oz/300ml guava juice

6 fl.oz/175ml Malibu

crushed ice

Keep two pineapple slices and chop the rest. Put the chopped pineapple with the juice from the tin and the gauva juice in a blender and blend until smooth. Pass through a sieve into a jug and add the Malibu. Stir well and pour into 4 tumblers. Chop the remaining pineapple rings and divide between the glasses. Add crushed ice to serve.

Bacardi and lime splash *(serves 4)*

2 tablespoons lime juice

1 rounded dessertspoon tamarind purée

2oz/50g granulated sugar

10 fl.oz/300ml boiling water

12 fl.oz/350ml sparkling mineral water

4 fl.oz/125ml Bacardi

crushed ice

4 lime slices

Put the lime juice, tamarind purée, sugar and boiling water into a jug and stir until the purée and sugar dissolve. Cover and refrigerate until cold. Add the sparkling mineral water and Bacardi and stir well. Pour into 4 tumblers and add crushed ice, and garnish each glass with a slice of lime.

Ginger and rum fizz *(serves 4)*

4oz/100g root ginger, peeled and finely chopped

10 fl.oz/300ml water

1oz/25g demerara sugar

16 fl.oz/475ml sparkling mineral water

4 fl.oz/125ml dark rum

ice cubes

4 pieces stem ginger

Bring the ginger, 10 fl.oz/300ml water and sugar to the boil, cover and simmer for 5 minutes. Leave to cool, then put in the fridge until cold. Strain into a jug and discard the ginger. Add the mineral water and rum and mix well. Pour into 4 tumblers and add some ice cubes. Thread the pieces of stem ginger onto cocktail sticks and use as garnish.

Tropical melon cocktail *(serves 4)*

8oz/225g ripe melon flesh, chopped

8 fl.oz/225ml sparkling mineral water

4 fl.oz/125ml tropical fruit juice

4 fl.oz/125ml Bacardi

crushed ice

Blend the melon flesh with the tropical fruit juice until smooth. Transfer to a jug with the water and rum and mix until well combined. Pour into 4 glasses and add crushed ice.

Ginger beer *(serves 6)*

40 fl.oz/1200ml boiling water

4oz/100g granulated sugar

¼oz/7g ground ginger

¼oz/7g cream of tartar

1 dessertspoon easy blend yeast

Put the sugar, ginger and cream of tartar in a large saucepan, add the boiling water and stir well. Cover and leave until lukewarm. Stir in the yeast, cover and allow to cool. Strain the mixture into a large jug, cover tightly and keep in the fridge overnight. Strain the beer into glasses, making sure not to disturb the sediment.

Melon and citrus cooler *(serves 4)*

1lb/450g ripe melon flesh, chopped

1 tablespoon lemon juice

1 tablespoon lime juice

1 tablespoon demerara sugar

12 fl.oz/350ml fresh orange juice

12 melon balls

crushed ice

4 orange slices

Blend the melon flesh, lemon, lime and orange juices and sugar until smooth. Refrigerate until cold, then whisk and pour into 4 glasses. Add 3 melon balls and some crushed ice to each glass and garnish the side with a slice of orange.

Lemon and lime cordial *(serves 4)*

> 2 tablespoons lemon juice
>
> 2 tablespoons lime juice
>
> 2oz/50g demerara sugar
>
> 10 fl.oz/300ml boiling water
>
> 20 fl.oz/600ml sparkling mineral water
>
> ice cubes
>
> lemon and lime slices

Mix the lemon and lime juice and sugar with the boiling water and stir until the sugar dissolves. Cover and put in the fridge until cold. Add the sparkling mineral water and mix well. Pour into 4 tumblers and add ice cubes and lemon and lime slices.

Peanut punch *(serves 4)*

> 32 fl.oz/950ml soya milk
>
> 4oz/100g smooth peanut butter
>
> gound cinnamon

Put the soya milk and peanut butter in a blender and blend until smooth. Pour into 4 tumblers and sprinkle the top with ground cinnamon.

Carrot and coconut refresher *(serves 4)*

8oz/225g carrots, scraped and grated

2oz/50g desiccated coconut

30 fl.oz/900ml water

ice cubes

Bring the carrot, coconut and water to the boil, cover and simmer for 5 minutes. Leave to cool, then refrigerate until cold. Strain the juice into a jug, pressing out as much liquid as possible. Stir well, pour into 4 glasses and add ice cubes.

Banana shake *(serves 4)*

12oz/350g ripe bananas, peeled and chopped

24 fl.oz/725ml soya milk

1 teaspoon vanilla essence

½ teaspoon ground cinnamon

crushed ice

Blend the banana with the soya milk, vanilla essence and ground cinnamon until smooth. Pour into 4 tumblers and add crushed ice.

More Vegan Cookbooks by Linda Majzlik

Vegan Dinner Parties

All the recipes are tried and tested. Although they are organised into monthly menus, you can of course pick and choose to make up menus and dishes for any occasion.

'Imaginative... very good value' *The Vegan*

'Linda's tasty book runs through the twelve months of the year with a mouth-watering and well-balanced three-course meal for each one' *Wildlife Guardian*

'This inspiring book proves just how sophisticated and tasty vegan food can be' *Agscene*

'Superb idea – a book long overdue' *Green World*

£5 paperback   96pp   1 897766 46 7

Vegan Barbecues and Buffets

Having a barbecue on a hot summer's day? Laying on a buffet for a crowded event? The vegan choice is simply great!

From mushroom and pine kernel sausages and smoked tofu and mushroom medallions, a sunflower and soya loaf and aubergine and brazil nut paté to a tempting assortment of salads, spreads and dips, and an array of sumptuous desserts, Linda Majzlik takes you on a festive journey of vegan delights that will appeal to every palate, yet remains completely wholesome and cruelty-free from beginning to end.

A lot of the preparation can be done in advance: many of the recipes are suitable for freezing, while others can be kept in the fridge. So the cook can enjoy the day as much as the guests...

£5 paperback   96pp   1 897766 55 6

Vegan Baking

Includes over 100 recipes for cakes, loaves, biscuits, tray bakes, no-bake cakes and savoury baking – all free of animal products and all tried and tested.

£5 paperback   96pp   1 897766 63 7

'The book that every vegan has been waiting for …
the kind of cookery book that you wouldn't get bored with …
a very useful addition to any kitchen.' *The Vegan*

A Vegan Taste of Italy

Starters, soups, sauces, risottos, main courses (including stuffed vegetables, pizza, pasta, and vegetables), salads and desserts, and baking (focaccia, bread-sticks, panforte, macaroons etc.). Over 120 recipes, with advice on maintaining a Caribbean storecupboard.

£5.99 paperback   128 pp   1 897766 65 3

Information on how to order can be found on the back of the title page of this book.